PSALM 34:14

SEEK PEACE AND PURSUE IT

53 $ 9.50 K

PSALM 34:14

Seek Peace and Pursue It

KENNETH L. MAXWELL

Foreword by
Edwin T. Dahlberg

Judson Press ® Valley Forge

Library of Congress Cataloging in Publication Data

Maxwell, Kenneth L.
  Seek peace and pursue it.

  Bibliography: p.
  Includes index.
  1. Peace (Theology) I. Title.
BT736.4.M35 1983   261.8'73   83-266
ISBN 0-8170-0992-2

Dedicated to

My Father and Mother

My Family

and

Peace for All of God's Human Family

Foreword

Anyone traveling around the world today is filled with sadness at the sight of military cemeteries on every continent. Row on row the white grave markers stretch to far horizons. In personal terms they remind us of wartime telegrams: "We regret to inform you. . . ." They speak to us of the heartbreak and tears of mothers, fathers, spouses, children, and sweethearts of those who died. These memories of two periods of human slaughter in our generation move us to seek to end war and pursue peace.

Today the very life of civilization is at stake. We have arrived at a stage in history in which a strong military defense may well prove to be the weakest defense—even obsolete. The debate as to whether the United States or Soviet Russia is the strongest military power is really beside the point. Both have sufficient power to destroy each other—multiplied many times by overkill—and to wipe out much of the human race. There are ominous dangers: of an accidental war (this threat increasing with nuclear proliferation), of terrorists holding governments at bay, of wars beginning within nations, and of anarchy. The more we spend for armament, the heavier the military taxation laid on the backs of people, the greater the danger of anarchy. This was the story of the downfall of the most powerful empires from Babylon to Rome to now. Are we so blind that we must follow that pathway to destruction? In the face of all this, who can escape the conviction that our most urgent mission now is the pursuit of peace?

That is what Kenneth Maxwell's book is all about. It deals with the conditions that make for peace, righteousness, and justice in relations of all races and nations; the biblical basis for this vast undertaking; and the hard thinking and work we must put into the task of organizing an effective world order.

Dr. Maxwell is well qualified to help us understand our mission as world citizens, individually and collectively. He is well aware that salvation is both personal and corporate. His extensive academic and theological education includes a Ph.D. from Yale University and studies at Woodrow Wilson School of Public and International Affairs, Princeton University; Colgate Rochester Divinity School; and Princeton Theological Seminary. He was also a Research Fellow at Yale University (1981–1982) and earlier a Graduate Research Scholar at Cambridge University in England.

His professional experience in practicing the pursuit of peace includes distinguished national and world leadership in the Christian church: in American Baptist and ecumenical circles through the National and World Councils of Churches.

He has authored articles, pamphlets, and contributions to books on peace. He coedited with Andrew W. Cordier, then at Columbia University, the Dag Hammarskjöld Memorial Lectures, second series, entitled *Paths to World Order.*

Action for peace by Dr. Maxwell, in which he has labored intensively, includes services as Executive Director of the Department of International Affairs of the National Council of Churches; Accredited Representative to the United Nations; consultant to Church World Service and the Division of Overseas Ministries, NCC. He gave leadership in the Commission of the Churches on International Affairs and in General Assemblies of the World Council of Churches in Evanston, New Delhi, and Uppsala. He directed two national conferences on World Order and two nationwide programs of Education and Action for Peace. He was instrumental, with other leaders, in founding the Church Center for the United Nations. He testified before numerous congressional committees and consulted with national and international officials around the world, including presidents, secretaries of state, foreign ministers, ambassadors, and other diplomats.

He has made valuable contributions to world understanding

in exchanges with church leaders and others in the Soviet Union, Germany, the United Kingdom, Latin America, Canada, Japan, Thailand, India, and the Middle East. He has circled the globe doing international research which has included firsthand observation in Yugoslavia, Romania, Hungary, Poland, East Germany, Czechoslovakia, and the Soviet Union as part of a fellowship project.

He was a delegate for UNICEF to the UN Conference on "The Human Environment" at Stockholm, in 1972; and as an observer for the United Nations Development Programme he was one of twenty scholars from around the world at the UNESCO Symposium on "Human Aggressiveness," Brussels.

His work for peace and justice includes serving as Chair and Professor of both the Political Science Department and Graduate Program for Administrators, Rider College, New Jersey; Visiting Professor at the School of Business Administration, Clarion State College, Pennsylvania; faculty member in the Political Science Department at Trenton State College, New Jersey; and lecturer in schools, colleges, universities and conferences across the U.S.A. and abroad.

In his teaching, writing, and other work, Dr. Maxwell is a living demonstration of his belief that education must be related to action, combining theory with practice, theology with life. Our time demands renewed emphasis on combining faith and work. I came to a deep appreciation of this linkage through a teacher and friend for whom I was privileged to serve as secretary, Professor Walter Rauschenbusch. Perennially, we need reemphasis on the scriptural imperative, echoed through the centuries by prophetic voices such as his, for faith to be at work.

This volume can be a valuable resource for study groups and workshops, in local churches, youth groups, universities, colleges, seminaries, denominational and ecumenical conferences.

I place special emphasis on its use at the local level in churches and community organizations. Helen Barrett Montgomery, the first woman to be elected president of the Northern (now American) Baptist Churches, was a foremost ecumenical leader, as far back as the 1920s. Famous for her New Testament translation, she traveled around the globe with women of many communions and nationalities for the world mission of the church. Yet she said that it is not enough for us to be a member of the church in general; we must be active members of a local church in particular. The importance of the local churches should be emphasized again now. Important also are *local* peace groups, schools, business and professional organizations, unions, and farm groups. We are too prone to look to the top echelons of our society for initiative in promoting world peace. It is at the grass roots level that the struggle for peace will be largely determined. Not one of us can afford to be neutral, uninformed, or disinterested. Each and all of us must wrestle with the crucial issues of this perilous time in light of our faith. We can do so in seminars and workshops based on this book. The cynics' chorus in our world may smile with amusement at the words of Jesus, "Blessed are the meek; for they shall inherit the earth," saying they are "naive" and "irrelevant." These cynics do not seem to realize that Jesus promised not that the meek would conquer, but that we should inherit the earth, as a result of "peacemaking."

Let us then leave the futile dreams of conquest to the past— to the Caesars, the Napoleons, the Hitlers, the Mussolinis, and the Stalins. The time has come to "seek peace—and pursue it," to redouble our efforts as peacemakers. Thus we can claim our inheritance, as children of God, to be shared with God's whole human family in a world at peace. The victory of God's kingdom is sure and everlasting.

Edwin T. Dahlberg

Contents

PSALM 34:14

SEEK PEACE AND PURSUE IT

Prologue

This book is written to communicate with you. It asks for your response, your thinking, and interacting with its message by your words and deeds as you work with others for peace.

The thrust of the book is summarized in the title, a challenge from the Bible: *"Seek Peace and Pursue It"* (Psalm 34:14; see also 1 Peter 3:11). In today's terms this could be stated "Work for Peace and Hang in There!"

Our theme can be summarized as working *in* Christian faith, hope, and love *for* peace with justice, freedom, and humanization.

We recognize that persons sharing similar objectives, such as peace, and common ties, such as citizenship or religion, may differ on international issues. Recently in the United States, debates have swirled around questions, such as SALT II, START, or not? Levels of armaments, up or down? Types of arms? In U.S.A.–U.S.S.R. relations: more confrontation or cooperation? In relations with the developing areas of the world: trade or aid, or both? Economic or military aid, or both; larger or smaller amounts of either; more bilateral or multilateral aid? More emphasis on military might, or on political, economic, and diplomatic initiatives? More concern for human rights here and around the world, or downgrading them? Continued depreciating of the United Nations, or renewal of U.S. leadership in international organizations for more global order?

The following example dramatizes how persons sharing common citizenship and religion can differ on world issues. During the "cold war" Secretary of State John Foster Dulles set forth a policy of "massive retaliation" for possible use of nuclear weapons. Dr. Edwin T. Dahlberg, a leader in the Christian ecumenical movement, called for a policy of "massive reconciliation." Fortunately, "massive retaliation" was not evoked. Some would say that the doctrine of "deterrence" worked. Others would emphasize that while "massive reconciliation" was not completed, at least openings were made in relations between the U.S.A. and the U.S.S.R. and between the U.S.A. and China, and breaking down "the iron curtain" and "the bamboo curtain" reduced threats of war.

Since wide differences of opinions are possible, readers are encouraged not necessarily to agree with what is in this book but to be stimulated in their own thinking and acting for peace.

A "Joint Venture"

Just as corporations share in a "joint venture" on an undertaking too gigantic for one alone, you and I, through this book, can share in a "joint venture."

The value of this volume will largely depend on your response. Emerson put the idea this way: "'Tis the good reader that makes the good book."[1] Menotti, the composer, speaking of the arts and people's response, said, "A book does not exist unless it is read. And it is not read unless the reader interacts."[2] Thus, you are invited to interact with the ideas of this book in a "joint venture" to "seek peace and pursue it," to increase your thinking and working for peace.

The Scope of Our Joint Venture

We focus in this book on the here and now. Our concerns include the U.S.A. and the wider world, their interdependence and interactions, in these critical years at the end of this century leading to a new millennium, at least in terms of the calendar. We concentrate on life-and-death issues of our time, on realities of the present, and on potentialities for the future in world affairs. We deal with a wide range of subjects: politics, economics, development, disarmament, social issues, race relations, human rights, U.S. foreign policy, the UN system, and other global and regional organizations in the public and private sectors. Related to such realities, we consider Christianity, the Bible, theology, ethics, church life and work, other religions, NGOs (nongovernmental organizations), and the life-styles of ourselves and other Christians, citizens, and peoples.

Churches and Peace

In our time there is most urgent need for more education and action by church organizations and their members in international relations. In past decades the churches have given vigorous leadership in programs for peace and related issues. Recent tides of rising concern by Christians give hope for renewal and enlargement of the work of the churches for peace. Currently, people at various levels—local, state, national, and world—in denominational, conciliar, interfaith, and broader coalitions are taking significant initiatives on such issues as disarmament, world economic and social development, hunger, human rights, and refugees. Of special significance are the recent actions of various denominations, including American Baptist Churches, the Protestant Episcopal Church, the United Church of Christ, the United Methodist Church, the United Presbyterian Church, U.S.A., and the Roman Catholic bishops to make "peace" a program priority. Of course, the historic peace churches, such as the Brethren, the Friends, and the Mennonites, persistently pursue peace as a priority.

In 1982, the National Council of Churches set a three-year program emphasis on "Peace with Justice" to coordinate priorities and to involve many other denominations in work for peace.

All these developments are encouraging, but *so much more* is needed if churches and Christians, and institutions and persons of other faiths, in the U.S.A. and around the world, are to begin to realize their potentials in relation to God's imperative to "seek peace and pursue it."

For Whom This Book Is Written

Potential readers are envisioned as including citizens in the general public who are interested in world affairs; faculty, administrators, campus ministers, undergraduate and graduate students in colleges, universities, and divinity schools; other youth and young adults; Christians and persons of other faiths interested in religious perspectives in relation to world issues; ecumenical and denominational officials and staff; pastors; and, especially, lay leaders and people of local churches. This latter group can use the book for individual self-education, study groups, and workshops. Pastors can use it in their preaching, teaching, programming, and leading in civic and ecumenical ministries for peace.

Is Peace Possible?

In such a world as ours and in light of some Bible passages a tough question faces us: "Is peace possible?" We address ourselves to that issue in theological and practical terms, looking at the most critical world problems and making suggestions of possible actions for working at them for more promise of peace.

"But What Can I Do?"

Another of the major questions we address is a widespread sense of powerlessness. Many people, confronted by the vast, complex forces of our time, have feelings of insignificance and of apathy, rooted in fear, frustration, and futility. They are overwhelmed by the BIGNESS of world problems, of government, of business, of labor, of education, of almost everything. They feel, "I have no say in what happens in our nation and the world."

By way of encouragement, we show that many people are doing more for peace than they may realize, as in supporting the Christian world mission and service programs. We consider types of education and action which have been effective in influencing global policies and developments.

We outline strategies available to us for acting through governmental and international channels. We also consider how we can gain more leverage in our work for peace by concerting our efforts through churches and other NGOs. We cite examples to show how *informed actions* by individuals and groups *can be important, can make a difference.*

We, as individuals—Christians, the faithful in other religions, citizens, members of the human race—are "bound in the bundle of life" with others, and are inextricably related to "the things that make for peace" . . . or for war.

Appropriate for "such a time as this"—the Nuclear/Space Age—for all of us who would be peacemakers is an interfaith "World Peace Prayer" (echoing St. Francis's simple prayer) being prayed daily by countless people around the globe:

Lead me from death to life, from falsehood to truth.
Lead me from despair to hope, from fear to trust.
Lead me from hate to love, from war to peace.
Let peace fill our heart, our world, our universe.

So, *you* are welcomed to enter into this "joint venture" for peace.
At its close, this book looks to the future with a question to
you.

Can We Survive
Until 2001 A.D. and Beyond?

"Would that even today you knew the things that make for peace! . . ."
(Luke 19:42)

We, the human race, are now on the list of "endangered species." We face threats from several sources. One is mass destruction by nuclear, biological, and chemical weapons. If we can avoid such universal disaster, still hundreds of millions of our kind face doom by other threats: poverty, malnutrition, starvation, disease, and early death.

Some observers doubt our prospects. For instance, one says that he must ask a question which is unvoiced but disturbs many: "Is there any hope for man?"

> In another era such a question might have raised thoughts of man's ultimate salvation or damnation. But today the brooding doubts that it arouses have to do with life on earth, now, and in the relatively few generations that constitute the limit of our capacity to imagine the future. For the question asks whether we can imagine that future other than as a continuation of the darkness, cruelty, and disorder of the past; worse, whether we do not foresee in the human prospect a deterioration of things, even an impending catastrophe of fearful dimensions.[1]

Other pessimistic voices have lamented that humankind had only one future—and that is now in the past. The seriousness of our situation is sharpened by the quip that amid questions about life on other planets we should be concerned with this issue: "Is there intelligent life on earth?" We can answer that, in part, by how we act on the life-and-death issues facing us now.

The urgency of effective action for survival is clear from scientists' reports on possible results of a nuclear war. Some are summarized by Jonathan Schell in *The Fate of the Earth*.[2] Most of us have a terrifying picture of the destruction of one city by one nuclear bomb. But Schell describes the results of a total attack with 10,000 missiles, of one megaton each. (It is generally reported that the U.S.S.R. has about 20,000 nuclear warheads and the U.S.A. about 30,000. So his case is conservative.) Across the U.S.A.,

> ... tens of millions of people would go up in smoke. ... as blast waves swept outward from thousands of ground zeros. ... substantially the whole human construct of the United States—would then be vaporized, blasted, or otherwise pulverized out of existence. ... substantial sections of the country [would be] turned ... into immense infernal regions ... from which escape is impossible.[3]

In most of the heavily populated areas of the U.S., "no one could escape alive." In remote areas a few might temporarily survive; but they would be subject to lingering death—lasting from days to months—by radiation. The areas where 60 percent of the people of the U.S.A. live would be totally destroyed by only three hundred bombs. This would leave 9,700, or 97 percent of the megatonnage of the attacking force to be used on overkill of that area and on the rest of the country.

> The statistics on the initial nuclear radiation, the thermal pulses, and the blast waves in a nuclear holocaust can be presented in any number of ways, but all of them would be only variations on a simple theme—the annihilation of the United States and its people.[4]

Those who speak of "civil defense," of transporting people to safer places, of "winning a nuclear war," or "recovery" after such a holocaust are not realists. "They are living in a past that has been swept away forever by nuclear arms."

> It has sometimes been claimed that the United States could survive a nuclear attack by the Soviet Union, but the bare figures on the extent of the blast waves, the thermal pulses, and the accumulated local fallout dash this hope irrevocably. They spell the doom of the United States. And if one imagines the reverse

attack on the Soviet Union, its doom is spelled out in similar figures.[5]

The wider impacts are stated by Schell in this way: ". . . a full-scale holocaust would, if it extended throughout the Northern Hemisphere, eliminate the civilizations of Europe, China, Japan, Russia, and the United States. . . ."[6] As to the effects of a nuclear attack on the rest of the planet and its people, we do not yet know enough to predict confidently what would happen. There is a strong likelihood that the world-around effects of radiation and other results of a thermonuclear war, including the impact on the ozone, might "shatter the ecological structure that permits man to remain alive on the planet." He concludes: "To say that human extinction is a certainty would, of course, be a misrepresentation—just as it would be . . . to say that extinction can be ruled out."[7] Schell concludes the first part of his presentation in this way:

> In trying to describe possible consequences of a nuclear holocaust, I have mentioned the limitless complexity of its effects on human society and on the ecosphere. . . . But if these effects should lead to human extinction, then all the complexity will give way to the utmost simplicity—the simplicity of nothingness. We—the human race—shall cease to be.[8]

Various futurologists are making projections ranging from bleak despair to measured optimism. Most agree that we humans can help to determine the course to doom or development. In this book we do not seek to foretell the future, whether humanity will survive until 2001 A.D., although we obviously hope so. Our task is to face the issue of survival as a responsibility of us all: to think and act to help our race live until 2001 A.D. and beyond.

Seeing Global Problems in Human Scale

Many of us feel a sense of futility in view of all the vast, complex problems related to world peace. They can seem so distant from our daily life, so complicated as to discourage comprehension, and so overwhelming as to paralyze capability for action. As a result, masses of people become apathetic and do not exercise their responsibilities as citizens. This is dangerous in a democracy based on "the consent of the governed." Problems worsen as our world reels from crisis to crisis.

One way to help us deal better with all this is to see global problems in human terms. This parallels the architectural idea of designing buildings and parts of massive cities to human scale. The aim is to make us feel less overwhelmed, more able to cope with life amid skyscrapers and the other tremendous masses in a megalopolis.

Global problems can be brought to human scale in two ways. First, we can realize that international relations are human relations. International problems—or progress—are caused by *human beings* and they harm—or help—*human beings*. To the point here is the concept, "international human relations," used in a report on "Peaceful Change in Modern Society."

> As we become more crowded on our planet, and as the newly developing nations begin to demand their rightful share of the world's resources, shortages . . . could feed the flames of old tribal rivalries unless humankind learns to apply . . . *international human relations.*[9]

A second way to bring global problems to human scale is to analyze these vast, complex realities into component parts so we can grasp them in our thinking and for our acting. We cannot reduce such tremendous problems to "bite size" and we must avoid oversimplification. But we can discern specific elements and see their relations to the whole picture. Thus we can think and act more effectively on world problems.

So let us consider some brief analyses of international relations. If this material is already familiar, it may be useful as a review as we prepare to deal with specific issues in later chapters.

Survival and the Quality of Life

In our analysis we see two related major concepts: "survival" and "the quality of life." Some politicians, and others, have oversimplified our world situation, saying, "*The* issue is survival." Obviously, survival is essential. But so is the quality of life. These two basic issues are so intertwined that they are difficult to separate at the global level. Billions of people suffer from such a lack of the quality of life that their survival is at stake. That involves us because the peace of the planet is inextricably related to the problems of the disadvantaged people of Earth.

"Survival" issues include the dramatic "doomsday" or "apocalyptic" questions: how to prevent nuclear war; how to moderate dangerously conflicting political, economic, and ideological forces; how to persist in working for arms control and reduction toward disarmament; how to deal with such concerns as "security," "defense," and military applications of science and technology. Some of these "survival" issues are related to the concept, in UN terms, of "peacekeeping."

"Quality of life" issues include less dramatic but also life-and-death questions for billions of our fellow human beings: Poverty, starvation, hunger, malnutrition, disease, and short life expectancy. It also applies to the broader economic, political, social, psychological, and ecological concerns, and includes the availability of energy and natural resources, peaceful uses of science and technology, and the full range of human rights and development. Such "quality of life" issues are related to the UN concept of "peace building."

People differ in their interests in the issues of "survival" or of the "quality of life." It is imperative that some concentrate on each, but that others work on both—all seeking peace.

The Kind of World We Live In

Another part of our analysis involves factoring out the major characteristics of international relations today. We are generally familiar with them, but restating them can serve us in developing our own thinking, in evaluating and seeking to influence U.S. foreign policy, and in setting our priorities for expenditures of thought, energy, time, and possessions in pursuing peace. It is hoped that each reader will think through his or her own summary of the major characteristics. As stimulus, the following are offered:

1. "Nuclear/Space Age"—shorthand for tremendous scientific and technological development with potentials for unprecedented destruction—or construction.
2. "Change"—rapid, accelerating, systemic, of revolutionary proportions around the globe.
3. A power struggle in so-called "East/West" terms between Communist-dominated areas and freedom-oriented areas of the world, including political, economic, ideological, social, and cultural dimensions, as well as military.

4. An increasing power struggle in so-called "North/South" terms between the "developed" and "developing" parts of the world, also involving all dimensions of relationships.

5. Growing nationalism *and* internationalism (a paradox).

6. More independence *and* interdependence (a paradox).

All these characteristics in combination make for new history; they present new challenges and they demand new responses.

The World "System" Today

Another approach in analysis is to examine international relations in terms of a system—or the lack of it.

The basic building blocks of the system are the nation states. All seek what they perceive to be their "national self-interest."[10] In a world of limited space and resources, conflicts are certain. So some people conclude that war is inevitable. But that does not necessarily follow. Conflicting interests are constantly contested in ways other than military, such as economic, political, psychological, cultural, and ideological.

So, basic questions confront us. What kinds of conflict are acceptable and practicable in our kind of world? What means exist or can be developed to channel, control, reconcile, or resolve various types of conflicts among nations? What attitudes, means, and machinery exist or can be invented for nations to (1) moderate their competition in pursuing "national self-interests" which conflict, and (2) increase their cooperation to further their coinciding interests and to promote human development of their citizens and of all peoples of Earth?

In analyzing world "systems" we have three basic options.

"Balance of Power" or "Power Politics"

In the "balance of power" or "power politics" concept, the leading nations seek to control events and resources for their "national self-interest" by influencing or coercing other nation states by all means available. Trying to maintain the balance of power, they seek to tilt it in their favor, for their maximum possible advantage, without precipitating armed conflict.

The concept of "power" needs to be conceived comprehensively. It is often thought of almost exclusively as military might. Sometimes political and economic factors are included. But it should be seen as also comprising other components:

ideological, psychological, social, cultural, and geographic realities; natural resources; population (negative if too small or too large in relation to other factors); education; religion (certain aspects); scientific-technological capabilites; and capacities for communication and transportation.

A classical "balance of power" model was that of the nineteenth century dominated by Britain. Nations deployed their power among competing states of Europe and colonies around the world in ways calculated to maintain stability in the system and to have it operate insofar as possible to their advantage.

Historically, the balance of power has been, at best, precarious. Shifts in its delicate equilibrium precipitated wars. With nations resorting to military might as the final arbiter, the nineteenth-century balance of power was blown apart by World Wars I and II. Since then, other, different "balances of power" have been tried, as will be discussed shortly.

"Collective Security"

A second conceptual system in international relations is "collective security." The Three Musketeers' motto "All for one and one for all" summarizes this system. It is a military system rather than a comprehensive one. All nations in the system agree to take action to oppose any nation attacking another.

No such system exists at the world level. Some call military alliances, such as NATO or the Warsaw Pact, "collective security." But these do not fit the classical definition. They are really parts of the "balance of power" model.

Some have called past and present international organizations "collective security." Woodrow Wilson referred to the League of Nations as such. Trygve Lie, the first secretary-general of the UN, characterized the UN as "collective security." But neither case meets the classical definition. There are *elements* of "collective security" in the UN Charter, such as Article 43, to establish permanent international military forces. But the member nations have not been willing to implement such plans. There have been *elements* of "collective security" in some UN operations. The joint action in Korea was the nearest to it. But this was not an advance undertaking; nor was it universal, being opposed by Communist-dominated nations.

In summary, "collective security," in the classical sense, has been and remains largely theory and not practice.

"Universal Order"

The third conceptual option for a system of international relations is that of "universal order." Various models are possible: a world federation developed on democratic principles; an order imposed by two or more "superpowers" on all other nations; world domination by one nation, or a group of persons, using international machinery to impose its will. The *1984* type of world in the last two models is obviously abhorrent and, fortunately, most difficult to effect.

At present we have no full-scale operation of the desirable concept of a democratic model of "universal order." There are embryonic beginnings in the UN system and in regional organizations. The most advanced model is the European community, moving from a supernational *toward* a supranational organization. The UN is neither of those. It is a loose confederation deriving its powers from voluntary cooperation of member nations, to a larger or smaller degree—usually the latter. (Regarding the UN, its nature, limitations, and potentials, see chap. 7.)

So we see in international relations only limited fractions of "universal order." However, within the UN system and regional organizations are potentialities, the beginnings of what can be developed toward a more rational, more peaceful, more just, and more humanizing "universal order."

A "System" of "International Anarchy"

We use the word "system" in quotation marks to emphasize that we do not have a rational one at the world level. What we have is suggested by Rube Goldberg's cartoons of disparate elements strangely interacting. It works somewhat; by fits and starts it jerks from crisis to crisis. Rather than a "system," it is, more realistically, relative "international anarchy."

A major concern around the world in the context of such a "system" is the new situation in history of "nuclear deterrence." It seems appropriate that it is referred to, in part, by the acronym MAD, short for "mutually assured destruction."

What we have on a global scale, then, is not a "universal order," nor "collective security," but largely a precarious, dangerous, life-threatening "balance of power." It is dominated by the most powerful nations in their own "national interest," as they perceive that.

Changing Models of "Balance of Power"

For a few years after World War II, the "balance of power" model was "bi-polarity," with the U.S.A. and its allies and the U.S.S.R. and its satellites dominating world affairs. Since the beginning of "the atomic age," in 1945, the two so-called "superpowers" have been developing increasingly sophisticated weapons of mass destruction, with increasing capacities for killing millions of people. Since the beginning of "the nuclear/space age," in 1957, they have been carrying out programs in space with military potentials and are piling up on Earth more arms for many times "overkill," seeking to maintain a precarious mutual deterrence, which Churchill described as a "balance of terror." They also keep adding to their other kinds of power, trying to weight the international balance to their own maximum advantage.

Events have moved the "system" toward "multipolarity."

First, more nations joined the nuclear club by developing such weapons, and a score of others gained the potential to do so. Thus, the two "superpowers" do not stand out so uniquely. Threats of mass destruction by mistake or madness are proliferating in a more complex pattern of terror.

Second, in political and economic terms, "multipolarity" or "polycentrism" developed. Allies and satellites of the two "superpowers" began to express diverging views, to assert varying degrees of independence, and to wield more world influence. Included were France, Yugoslavia, Albania, the People's Republic of China, and other nations in Latin America, Africa, and Asia.

Third, doctrines stressing almost exclusively preeminence of military might and nuclear prowess, in particular, began to fade with the U.S.A.–Vietnam experience, the Iranian bondage, and the U.S.S.R.–Afghanistan misadventure. Questions about limits of the effectiveness of armed force are increasing. Recognition of the importance of other types of power is beginning to grow.

Fourth, the developing areas, with by far the majority of nations, are seeking a larger share of leadership in world affairs. OPEC (Organization of Petroleum Exporting Countries) offers a dramatic example; its impact is reverberating around the world in terms of energy, and consequent economic, political, diplomatic, social, and military effects. Another significant sign of the dispersion of power is the increasing role of growing numbers of "developing nations" in the UN system, international conferences, and events. They are demanding a "new economic order" and other developments to promote their "national interest," which they generally see as coinciding with the "world's interest."

Some Basic Questions

The present "balance of power" with its changing models poses fundamental questions: What security can "nuclear deterrence" ultimately offer? How long can nuclear arms keep proliferating without exploding into war? What are the costs— financial, but especially human—of the present "system"? What are its impacts on the "superpowers" and other nations as to a sense of security and as to economic and social development? What realistic alternatives are there?

In summary, a most crucial issue, "survival," with a constellation of complexities, confronts the human race: How can we maintain through necessary transition the "balance of power," preventing war, while moving from this relatively irrational, anachronistic, anarchistic lack of "system" toward a more intelligent, interdependent "universal order"?

The urgency of this question is clear. A thermonuclear conflict would destroy civilization and possibly the human race. This is underscored in the stark statement by a former U.S. Department of Defense official, Herbert Scoville, now heading the Arms Control Association. In reply to former Secretary of State Haig's erroneous claim of a NATO option of a nuclear explosion to warn the U.S.S.R. against hostilities in Europe, Scoville warned that would lead to nuclear war. Result? "No Europe left, no Soviet Union left, no United States left."[11]

In summary, another crucial question, related to the "quality of life," with a constellation of complexities, confronts us: How can we make all the momentous national and international moves to change the present world of disorder, with its vast, needless pain, suffering, and sorrow, to a new order with more justice, freedom, and human development?

The urgency of this question is clear when we see the economic and social disparities of life-and-death impact. A minority of the globe's people live in plenty (resulting in obesity for some), luxury, comfort, knowledge, and health, with increasing life spans while the vast majority of our race are ill-fed, ill-clothed, ill-housed, illiterate, ill, and facing early death.

We consider steps toward meeting these basic issues in the conclusion of this chapter and in succeeding ones.

Getting at the Causes of War—AND of Peace

During the Vietnam conflict came news reports that peace might "break out." This suggested peace as spontaneous and depending on fortunes of war. But are there *causes* of peace?

We are accustomed to thinking about the causes of war. Empirical, comprehensive studies have been made.[12] They show that wars usually have several causes, that these are related, and that the importance of these factors differ from case to case. Some have tried, unsuccessfully, to cite one cause for wars; for example, Marxism attributed wars to economic conflicts of capitalism. The inadequacy of that explanation is evident from centuries of wars before capitalism. Obviously, the economic factor has been one of the major causes of war. But it is not the only one. Nations have gone to war for other primary reasons, sometimes even though it was against their economic interests. Nationalistic or "patriotic" hysteria has driven nations to war, ignoring economic interest. In the face of history, any simplistic ideology of causes of war defaults to multifactored analysis.

A listing of major causes of wars through the centuries includes (in alphabetical order): arms, culture, economics, ideology, language, nationalism, politics (internal and external), power (striving to get, keep, or wield it), psychology (personal and social), race, religion (some kinds of), resources, science, and territory.

Accustomed to thinking of the "causes of war," many do not think of the "causes of peace." But as surely as war is caused, so peace must be caused. Peace is more than cessation of armed conflict, the "absence of war." Peace, as we define it later, comprises positive, dynamic realities in the lives of individuals, groups, nations, and the world.

It is heartening that increasing numbers of people and in-

stitutions around the globe are devoting themselves to war/
peace studies, to thinking, researching, writing, and teaching
about the causes of peace as well as war. Peace institutes in
many countries are probing these issues.[13] These institutes are
significant in developing data, providing proposals for public
policy, and creating informed "peacemakers." "Peace studies"
are increasing in the curricula of colleges and universities.
However, still more extensive and combined efforts are needed
to recognize, analyze, and remove the "causes of war," and to
recognize, analyze, and develop the "causes of peace."

Our Time and the "Conditions of Peace"

A concept related to the "causes of peace" is expressed in the
phrase "conditions of peace." This phrase encompasses ideas,
attitudes, relationships, and realities in political, economic,
social, and other dimensions of life which are conducive to
creating, maintaining, and increasing peace.

This idea of the "conditions of peace" is to be found in the
thinking of Jesus, and in ways which have meaning for our
time. On his last journey to Jerusalem, as Jesus came in sight
of the city, he wept over it, lamenting, "Would that even today
you knew the things that make for peace!" (Luke 19:41-44).
This sentence is translated by Goodspeed in these words: "If
you yourself only knew today the conditions of peace!"

But then, Jesus sadly prophesied that disaster would come
upon Jerusalem (its name meaning, ironically, "possession of
peace") because its people were not aware of the life-and-death
issues facing them and were not concerned with peace. He said
destruction would come "because you did not know the time of
your visitation." Total destruction did come within a generation.

Do we recognize "the time of our visitation" as a nation and
as a world? We live in such a "time." *Kairos* is the New Testament Greek term; it has a profound theological meaning
which is a God-given time that confronts us with decisions and
actions making for peace or for annihilation.

Kairos can mean, if we grasp the opportunities, a time of
promise; if we ignore them, a time of doom. The U.S.A., other
nations, and the world are now confronted with unprecedented
crises, with more dangers and more opportunities than in all
history! Such a time, this *kairos*, demands our awareness, con-

cern, and action. The problems, if we neglect them, can overwhelm the promise, and we and our world can go down in disaster. The promise, if we work effectively on the problems, holds the prospect for a more abundant life for all humankind. The challenge from the Bible confronts us now: Are we concerned about the "conditions of peace"? Will we study them and act to create more of them? Do we, will we, "seek peace and pursue it"?

These questions bring us to the final issue in this chapter.

The Decision Makers re "Survival" and "Quality of Life"

Human survival until 2001 A.D. and the quality of life will be determined, under God and God's purposes, by governments, international institutions, political, economic and social leaders, nongovernmental organizations, including churches especially, and "we, the people," who can be an increasing force for peace, *if we will.*

Will the other decision makers—and we:

See international problems in human scale?

Be concerned with "survival" *and* the "quality of life"?

Understand the characteristics of our world?

Move from a "balance of power" toward "universal order"?

Seek to eliminate causes of war and promote causes of peace?

Work to create the "conditions of peace"?

How "we, the people," NGOs, other leaders, governments, and international institutions deal with such questions—by our action or inaction—will help to determine in this time, this *kairos,* whether, and how well, we and our world may survive until 2001 A.D. and beyond.

What Does the Bible Say to Us About Peace?

> Let me hear the words of the LORD:
> are they not words of peace . . .?
> (Psalm 85:8, *New English Bible*)

The Bible has been the basis for differing beliefs and actions among Christians. In World War II, General Patton prayed: "God of our Fathers, who by land and sea has ever led us to victory, please continue your inspiring guidance in this the greatest of our conflicts. . . . Grant us the victory, Lord."[1] Such Americans were joined by British, French, and Russian Christians praying for victory. On the other side, German Christians were praying to the same God, in the tradition, *"Gott mit uns."* They were joined by Italian and other Christians. After prayers, millions of Christians killed millions of fellow Christians and others, on both sides. Other Christians, because of their faith based on the Bible, refused to participate in war. Many Christians on all sides, because of their faith based on the Bible, were praying for everybody suffering from war, even "enemies," and for the earliest end to the human slaughter. Prayer such as the latter is referred to in words inscribed at the Church Center for the UN: "THE GREATEST PRAYER OF MAN DOES NOT ASK FOR VICTORY BUT FOR PEACE."[2]

In face of such differing views about God, religion, prayer, war, and peace, it is important to examine what the Bible, with its authority for faith and life, may say to us about these subjects. A full exploration would fill volumes.[3] Here we can 35

only briefly focus on various understandings of the nature of
God with corresponding responses expected from believers, as
seen in different parts of the Bible, then draw some conclusions.
We do not have space to discuss methodology, but we do take
account of the findings of biblical scholarship.

One crucial question is how we use the Bible. Have you heard
people cite one or more isolated verses to try to prove a point?
Often they do not take account of verses with differing meanings, and they pick verses out of context. For example: "Blessed
be he who seizes your little ones, and dashes them to pieces
upon a rock!" "Go, and do thou likewise" (Psalm 137:9, Goodspeed; Luke 10:37b, KJV). That proof-text method is not persuasive, nor does it respect the integrity of the Bible. By contrast, our approach is to see major concepts in the Bible, in
context, relate them to each other, and discern meanings for
us.

"The Lord, Mighty in Battle"

In the Old Testament there is much bloody theology and
interpretation of history. Most of this centers upon the por-
trayal of the LORD, Yahweh,[4] as a "God of war." Pervading the
accounts of earlier history are concepts of "the LORD, mighty
in battle," "the LORD of hosts" (Hebrew for "armies"),[5] the LORD
"delivering the enemies" to his people, and the total destruction
of enemies in "holy war" (in Hebrew, ḥerem).[6]

The following concepts parallel those of other cultures at
that time. Their territory belonged to a god who protected it
and them. A warrior, their god went with them into battle as
they carried his symbol before them. (A precursor of later
armies' ensigns and flags?) Thus, the Israelites carried the ark
of the covenant before their army, as in the battle of Jericho
(Joshua 6). God commanded them to make "holy war" totally
to destroy enemies.

We find seven variations on the theme of Yahweh as a war
God:

1. Yahweh of armies, LORD of hosts, versus enemies of his
people, in the violence of the Exodus from Egypt and of the
invading conquest of Canaan (Exodus, Deuteronomy, Joshua,
Judges).

2. Yahweh, the warrior, engaging in hand-to-hand combat
with the enemies of the believers (some psalms).

3. Yahweh, caught in a dilemma of whom to fight for when his people divided in two, Judah and Israel, and seen as aiding the one more faithful to him (Kings and Chronicles).

4. Yahweh, fighting against his own people, using enemy nations as his agents of destruction to punish them for their unfaithfulness (Joshua, Judges, Kings, Chronicles, Prophets).

5. Yahweh, becoming so wrathful against both his own people and their enemies that he brings destruction on all! (Prophets).

6. Yahweh, warning his people not to enter alliances but to put their trust in him as their protector (Some prophets).

7. Yahweh, promising to fight for his people *but* commanding them *not* to engage in war (some psalms and Prophets).

Discussion of such subjects fills volumes.[7] Here we must limit ourselves to sample references. Yahweh, war God, speaks: "I will send my fear before thee, and *will destroy all the people to whom thou shalt come ...*" (Exodus 23:27, KJV, author's emphasis). The marching orders are to be delivered by the priest before battle. (A precursor of chaplains?) "When you go forth to war ... *the LORD your God is with you ...* "*the LORD your God is he that goes with you, to fight for you against your enemies, to give you the victory*" (Deuteronomy: 20:1-4, author's emphasis). Yahweh had star war powers, with his "heavenly hosts": "They fought from heaven; the stars in their courses fought against Sisera" (Judges 5:20, KJV, "The Song of Deborah"). Yahweh also waged psychological warfare: "For *it was the LORD'S doing to harden their hearts* [peoples in Canaan who would not surrender] that they should come against Israel in battle, *in order that they should be utterly destroyed, and should receive no mercy but be exterminated ...*" (Joshua 11:20, author's emphasis).

At the command of this war God, and in his name, savagery is rife; gory stories of murders, assassinations, and beheadings, as well as bloody battles, abound. All are presented as works *by* or *for* Yahweh. (The reader can explore further if he or she has the stomach for it and a desire to know more about this war God and the bloodbaths wrought by Yahweh or by his people in his name. WARNING: These stories of violence, as those on TV, may become morbidly fascinating.) Yahwistic bloodiness flows in the stories of Phinehas (Numbers 25:6-18), Ehud (Judges 3:15-31), Deborah and Barak (Judges 4), Gideon

(Judges 7–8), Jephthah (Judges 11–12), Samson (Judges 13–16), Samuel (1 Samuel 1–25); Saul (1 and 2 Samuel), David (1 and 2 Samuel) and succeeding kings too many even to mention (Kings and Chronicles).

In the Psalms, usually thought of as devotional, there is much exalting of a God of war, wrath, and destruction. Of 150 psalms, more than 80 have such violent strains. For instance, Psalm 137 evokes compassion for Israel in captivity, weeping by the rivers of Babylon, but then comes cursing against that land, and the blessing which would be expected from God for its destroyers, with this climax: Happy shall he be who picks up your babies by the heels and smashes their brains out on a rock. (Contrast Jesus pronouncing woe on any who would offend a child and taking children in his arms and blessing them: "of such is the kingdom of God" [Luke 17:2; Mark 10:13-16, KJV; and parallels].) Bloodthirstiness abounds in the Psalms; for example, bloody Yahweh is seen slaughtering others "That thy foot may be dipped in the blood of *thine* enemies, *and* the tongue of thy dogs in the same" (Psalm 68:23, KJV, author's emphasis). With such a background, Psalm 24:8-10 which we innocently use as liturgy, may be seen as originally being a salute to the war God:

> Who is this King of glory?
>   The LORD (Yahweh), strong and mighty,
>   The LORD (Yahweh), mighty in battle. . . .
>
> Who is this King of glory?
> The LORD of hosts (Yahweh of armies),
>   he is the King of glory!

Many bloody passages about the works of the God of war are found in the Prophets (Amos, Isaiah, Joel). A most vivid one is the slaughter forecast by God via Ezekiel (39:17-20).

This Yahweh is seen as not only condoning but also causing ultimate savagery and degradation, in most revolting scenes; he threatens that he will make his people eat the fruit of their own body, the flesh of their sons and daughters, and other members of their own family! (Deuteronomy 28:53 ff.)

This vengeful, wrathful, bloodthirsty war God, who is "mighty in battle," is withal a "happy warrior." He *delights* in dealing out death and destruction, as well as in doing good. This is obvious in scenes where he is slaughtering the enemies of his people, but it is true when he slaughters as well: ". . . as the LORD took delight in doing you good and multiplying you, so the LORD will take *delight* in bringing ruin upon you and destroying you . . ." (Deuteronomy 28:63, author's emphasis). (Contrast with a prophetic view, as in Micah 7:18, where, ultimately, God "delights in mercy.")

This Yahweh, God of war, is to be hailed by the believers: "'For the LORD your God is God of gods, and Lord of lords, the great, *the mighty, and the terrible God* . . .'" (Deuteronomy 10:17, author's emphasis).

How are believers to respond to such a God? They are to show to those who are not believers anger, hatred, and vengefulness, (see many psalms, such as, 139:19-22) delighting in enemies' deaths: "The righteous shall rejoice when he seeth the vengeance: he shall wash his feet in the blood of the wicked" (Psalm 58:10, KJV). God's people's duty? To wage "total war" with "no pity": "And *you shall destroy all the peoples that the LORD your God will give over to you,* your eye shall have *no pity upon them*" (Deuteronomy 7:16, author's emphasis; last phrase from KJV).

In outlying cities, they are to kill all males and ". . . enjoy the spoil [women, children, and everything else] of your enemies, which the LORD your God has given you" (Deuteronomy 20:14). Cities in "the promised land" they are to destroy totally! (See Deuteronomy 20:16-18.)

> "You shall not be in dread of them; for the LORD your God is in the midst of you, a great and terrible God. The LORD your God will clear away these nations before you . . . the LORD your God will give them over to you, and *shall destroy them with a mighty destruction, until they be destroyed*" (Deuteronomy 7:21-23, author's emphasis; last phrase from KJV. The Hebrew construction reflected here piles up tremendous impact).

The believers are to kill until there are mountainous body counts: one hundred thousand Syrians in one day! (1 Kings 20:29); Judah slaying "five hundred thousand chosen men" of Israel (2 Chronicles 13:17, KJV); one million, "an host of a thousand thousand," Ethiopians "were destroyed before the LORD" (2 Chronicles 14:9-13, KJV).

"Here endeth the lesson" about Yahweh, "the LORD mighty in battle," and the believers' duty to bring destruction and death.

The Lord of Life

In contrast to Yahweh, warring LORD of destruction and death, more generally throughout the Bible God is seen as the Lord of life, the Creator, Giver, and Sustainer of life.

In the creation story God is seen as breathing the breath of life into humankind and bringing forth all the teeming life of the universe (Genesis 1–2). Some psalms refer to different aspects of God, the Lord of life (16:11; 21; 23; 27; 66).

In the New Testament, Jesus, the incarnate Word, becomes central for life, and life eternal. The Gospel of John in its opening fanfare declares that "in him was life; and the life was the light of men" (1:4). Jesus used the following idea for the sustaining of life: "I am the bread of life." In a meditation on the Eucharist, the Lord's Supper, in which that simile occurs, Thomas à Kempis praises the "Creator and giver of life to all spirits."[8]

Jesus declared: "'I am the way, and the truth, and the life'" (John 14:6); that he had come so people "might have life, and . . . have it more abundantly" (John 10:10, KJV); that "God so loved the world, that he gave his only begotten Son, that whosoever believeth in him should not perish, but have everlasting life" (John 3:16, KJV); "'I am the resurrection and the life . . . and whoever lives and believes in me shall never die'" (John 11:25-26).

Jesus is praised as the one who "brought life and immortality to light . . ." (2 Timothy 1:10).

As for the response of the believers, Jesus says that they are to follow in his way and he will give them "'the light of life'" (John 8:12). Paul indicates by his own experience that believers are to live in such a way that Jesus Christ lives in them (Galatians 2:20). They are to endure all manner of tribulation that the life of Jesus might be made manifest in them (2 Corinthians 4:8-12). A believer is to love, honor, respect, and serve the life of others, even to the extent of being willing to give one's life for the sake of the life of others (John 13–17; 15:13; et al.). (Note: This does not say to kill others for one's friends.) A modern disciple, Albert Schweitzer, carries the thought of the believer's response to the Lord of life to its logical conclusion. He commends as the centerpiece of philosophy and practice, "reverence for life."[9]

The believers are to follow the way of life, not of death. Moses assembled the Israelites for his farewell address. The Bible says that he spoke the words which came from God. In that dramatic setting, toward the close of his message are these words: "See, I have set before thee this day life and good, and death and evil. . . . I have set before you life and death, blessing and cursing: therefore choose life, that both thou and thy seed may live. . . . he (the LORD) is thy life" (Deuteronomy 30:15-20, KJV). This concept of "the Lord of life" is relevant to seeking peace. On Peace Sabbath, May 30, 1982, churches across the U.S.A. had this focus for worship, study, and action. Thus, "the Lord of life" is seen as speaking to us in this perilous, nuclear age: "See, I have set before thee this day life and good, and death and evil. . . . choose life. . . ."

"The God of Peace"

"O sing unto the LORD a new song" can have special meaning when we see it praising the Lord God of peace not of war (Psalms 33:3; 96:1). This theme finds cosmic roots in the beginning, when "God created the heavens and the earth" (Genesis 1:1 ff.). Out of chaos God brought order. Surely, the God great enough to create the earth can bring peace on it. This assumption underlies the new song in Psalms.

In both Psalms and Prophets there is growing understanding of God as the stopper of war and the maker of peace:

> He makes wars to cease to the end of the earth;
>   he breaks the bow, and shatters the spear,
>   he burns the chariots with fire! (Psalm 46:9)

> His abode has been established in Salem ["Peace"]. . . .
> There he broke the flashing arrows,
>   the shield, the sword, and the weapons of war (Psalm 76:2-3).

> Let me hear what God the LORD will speak,
>   for he will speak peace to his people (Psalm 85:8a),
>   . . . but let them not turn again to folly (Psalm 85:8b, KJV).

There is a "glory" of peace superseding the "glory" of war, with love, fidelity, truth, righteousness, and prosperity (Psalm 85:9-13; cf. Psalms 29, 72). God's promise of peace pervades the Prophets (e.g., Isaiah 54:10; 55:12-13; Ezekiel 34:25). A new covenant of perpetual peace is related to the order of creation. Hosea quotes the God of peace: ". . . I will break the bow and the sword and the battle out of the earth, and will make them to lie down safely" (2:18, KJV). In Isaiah with all its threats of destruction by Yahweh (on his people if they do not repent, or if they do, on their enemies), he wills peace (26:12). God says, "'Behold, I am doing a new thing'" (43:19), and his people's "warfare is ended" (40:2). Now, Isaiah's vision of the peace of God among nations is chiseled on the UN Plaza for all the world to see and strive for:

> . . . they shall beat their swords into plowshares,
>   and their spears into pruning hooks;
> nation shall not lift up sword against nation,
>   neither shall they learn war any more (Isaiah 2:4).

In his prophecy, "For unto us a child is born, unto us a son is given," referring to the "Prince of Peace," he describes the future:

> Of the increase of his government and of peace
>   there will be no end . . .
> with justice and with righteousness
>   from this time forth and for evermore.
> The zeal of the LORD of hosts will do this (Isaiah 9:7).

Isaiah paints in words several pictures of "The Peaceable Kingdom."[10] God's Messiah will be peaceable and gentle (42:3). God's messenger will bring "the good news" of prosperity and peace: "How beautiful upon the mountains are the feet of him who brings good tidings, who publishes peace" (52:7; see Acts 10:36 about Jesus "preaching the good news of peace.").

Isaiah contrasts the old order of war and the new order of peace:

> I am the LORD . . . which bringeth forth the chariot and the horse,
> the army and the power; they shall lie down together, they shall
> not rise: *they are extinct.* . . . Remember ye not the former things,
> neither consider the things of old. Behold, I will do a new thing
> . . . (43:15-21, KJV).

Then follow a promise and a vision of God's peace. Repeatedly, the prophet proclaims God's purpose and covenant of peace, "and great shall be the peace of thy children," (Isaiah 54:13b, KJV).

What does the God of peace require? His people are to pray for God's "saving health among all nations" (Psalm 67:2). They are to put their trust not in armies, chariots, and horses (Psalms 20, 33, etc.), not in military alliances (Isaiah 30, 31, etc.), but in God, in his salvation, and in his promises for peace (Isaiah 25, 32, 33, 55, etc.; Psalms 62, 91, 121, etc.). They are to revere the LORD and "walk in his ways" if they wish to see peace (Psalm 128). They are to "seek peace, and pursue it" (Psalm 34:14).

The pursuit of peace through wisdom gives a beautiful model of conflict resolution in Genesis 13 (KJV). Abram and Lot prospered; their flocks and people increased until "the land was not able to bear them." The population explosion meant strife.

> ... Abram said to Lot, "Let there be no strife between you and me, and between your herdsmen and my herdsmen; for we are kinsmen. Is not the whole land before you? Separate yourself from me. If you take the left hand, then I will go to the right; or if you take the right hand, then I will go to the left." ... thus they separated from each other (Genesis 13:8-9,11b).

After that peaceful settlement, the LORD, pleased with Abram's action, promised him blessings of lands and descendants.

Pursuing peace through wisdom is counseled in the Wisdom Literature, with theology implicit and advice prudential (Proverbs 15:1; Ecclesiastes 7:19; 10:4). One story is a gem:

> I have also seen this example of wisdom under the sun, and it seemed great to me: There was a little city with few men in it; and a great king came against it and besieged it. ... But there was found in it a poor wise man, and he by his wisdom delivered the city. ... I say that wisdom is better than might. ... Wisdom is better than weapons of war ... (Ecclesiastes 9:13-18).

In the New Testament, "the God of peace" reigns, with Jesus Christ as the "Prince of Peace." There are practically no traces of "the God of war." There are *no* calls to bloody battles, *only* to peace. Even the Revelation, after apocalyptic conflicts, moves to resolution in peace, in the new heaven and the new earth, for ever and ever. Everywhere, God's peaceful nature is clear; in one blessing, God is described as *"the very God of peace"* (1 Thessalonians 5:23, KJV).

Almost all New Testament letters have salutations of "peace" related to God; several have similar benedictions. They are more than formalities; they have theological significance. They constantly proclaim "the God of love and peace." The Hebrew greeting "Shalom," a part of Jewish custom, is rich in meanings: *peace,* order, well-being, health, wholeness, salvation. There is added significance in these salutations and benedictions because they combine "love" or "grace," terms having theological meaning, with "peace." Further, these blessings have an additional direct theological connection in that they are usually invoked "from God the Father and the Lord Jesus Christ."

The nature of the Father is seen in constant references to "the God of peace" (e.g., Romans 1:7; 15:33; 16:20; 1 Corinthians 1:3; 2 Corinthians 1:2; Galatians 1:3; Ephesians 1:2; Philippians 1:2; Colossians 1:2; 1 Thessalonians 1:1; 5:23; 2 Thessalonians 1:2; Philemon 3; Hebrews 13:20-21; 1 Peter 1:2; 2 Peter 1:2; 3:14; 2 John 1:3).

It would follow that the Son would also partake of that nature of peace. This is indicated by Paul in a passage in which he repeatedly refers to Jesus Christ as "Lord," and concludes with a comprehensive benediction from "the Lord of peace": "Now may the Lord of peace himself give you peace at all times in all ways . . ." (2 Thessalonians 3:16).

What is the response expected from believers to "the God of peace" and to "the Lord of peace"? According to Jesus, the central response is to "love God" and to "love your neighbor as yourself" (Matthew 22: 36-40). Having faith, they "ought always to pray and not lose heart" (Luke 18:1; cf. Matthew 7: 7-8; 21:21-22). This counsel is most relevant for those who are to "seek peace *and pursue it*," in face of disappointments, discouragements, and the enormity of it all! How to pray is suggested in the model given by Jesus in "the Lord's Prayer," which includes a specific petition for God's kingdom to come and God's will to be done on earth (Matthew 6:9-13). Seeking to help fulfill such prayers in their lives and in the life of the world, and knowing that "wars and fightings" come from selfish motives "warring" within us, believers are to seek the "wisdom from God" which is "peaceable, gentle, open to reason, full of mercy" (James 3:17). What is the result? "The harvest of righteousness is sown in peace by those who make peace" (James 3:18). "Let the peace of Christ rule in your hearts" is another counsel to Christians (Colossians 3:15). ". . . God's call is a call to live in peace" is applied to family life (1 Corinthians 7:15, *New English Bible*). In church life, "all things" are to "be done decently and in order," "for God is not a God of confusion but of peace" (1 Corinthians 14:40, 33).

Believers are to live in love, forgiveness, reconciliation, and peace with all men, insofar as that depends on them (Matthew 22:39; 6:14-15; 1 Corinthians 13; Ephesians 4:32; Colossians 3:13; Matthew 5:22-24; 2 Corinthians 5:17-20; Romans 12:18; Hebrews 12:14; 1 John 2, 3, 4). They are to "keep the commandments" (John 14:15; 1 John 3:22; 2 John 6). They are to "do good works" (James 2, 3, 4). These are set forth in lists, which often include seeking peace. Paul writes:

> ... be at peace with all men, if possible, so far as that depends on you. ...
> *if your enemy is hungry, feed him,*
> *if he is thirsty, give him drink;*
> *for in this way you will make him*
> *feel a burning sense of shame.*
> Never let evil get the better of you; get the better of evil by doing good (Romans 12:18-21, Moffatt).

Similar to that is a passage in 1 Peter 3:8-11:

> Finally, all of you, have unity of spirit, sympathy, love of the brethren, a tender heart and a humble mind. Do not return evil for evil or reviling for reviling; but on the contrary bless. ... "... let him turn away from evil and do right; let him seek peace and pursue it."

That quotation from Psalm 34 underscores that the same response to the God of peace is expected in both the Old and New Testaments. And "the God of peace" gives peace to those who "live in peace": "Mend your ways ... agree with one another, live in peace, and the God of love and peace will be with you" (2 Corinthians 13:11).

"Peace" in the New Testament is sometimes limited to the Christian community. But for many, that encompassed their world. However, Jesus' ideas go beyond that circle, to Samaritans (Luke 10:30-37; John 4:5-30), to Romans (Matthew 5:41; 8:5 ff.), even to "enemies" (Matthew 5:38-41, 43-48). Various epistles specify that "peace" is to reach out to "all" (Romans 12:18; Hebrews 12:14). The overarching reality is that the God of love revealed in Jesus Christ is the God of all people and indeed of the cosmos, the universal God of peace. (For more on this see chapter 4 on "Love and Peace?")

"The Lord Is My Shepherd"

Alongside the concept of "the God of peace," also contrasting with Yahweh, the God of war, is God, the good shepherd. He is the LORD of lovingkindness, steadfast love, and tender mercies. Occasionally we see such qualities of God in the Pentateuch and historical books (Numbers 14:18; 2 Chronicles 30:9; Nehemiah 9:17). Such ideas are central in the Psalms and the Prophets. In a most beloved passage of Scripture, Psalm 23, the LORD is the shepherd, caring for the believer through the needs and crises of life. More than a score of Psalms refer to the Shepherd God. Certain prophets portray God as the good shepherd, and his peaceful Messiah likewise (Isaiah 40; Ezekiel 34). This Shepherd God was sometimes seen as combining might with mercy, protecting his people, but not summoning them to war (Psalm 2; Isaiah 40; Ezekiel 34).

The merciful LORD calls his people to live in peace: "Cease from anger, and forsake wrath" (Psalm 37:8, KJV); "seek righteousness, seek meekness" (Zephaniah 2:3, KJV; Psalm 25:9). In earlier history accounts, God was thought to bless especially the conquering, military leaders; the new emphasis is, oppositely, on "the meek" (Psalm 147, esp. 6, 10-11, 14). We see this again in Psalm 37:11 (KJV) which Jesus made a beatitude in his teaching and in his life: "But the meek shall inherit the earth; and shall delight themselves in the abundance of peace." Isaiah shows God and his Messiah concerned for the meek:

> The Spirit of the Lord GOD is upon me;
> because the LORD hath anointed me
> to preach good tidings unto the meek (61:1, KJV).

Significantly, Jesus identified himself with that role of the Messiah (Luke 4:16-21) and as the good shepherd (John 10, esp. vv. 11, 14-18). In contrast to a conquering military Messiah, Jesus said, in keeping with the "Suffering Servant" concept in Isaiah, "'I lay down my life for the sheep'" (John 10:17). When asked whether he was the Messiah, Jesus replied in the scriptural image of the shepherd and the sheep (John 10:24-30). In the parable of "the good shepherd," Jesus spoke of his ministry (Luke 15:1-7; see Matthew 10:6; Ezekiel 34). "The God of peace," "the shepherd," and "the covenant" are joined in a benediction:

> Now may the God of peace who brought again from the dead our Lord Jesus, the great shepherd of the sheep, by the blood of the eternal covenant, equip you with everything good that you may do his will, working in you that which is pleasing in his sight . . . (Hebrews 13:20-21).

Good works in meekness were required to do the will of the Shepherd Lord. Such meekness is not to be confused with weakness. It possesses power such as enabled the early followers of Jesus to be "more than conquerors" (Romans 8:37) and to be those who "turned the world upside down" (Acts 17:6). (That language of opponents we might reverse to say, "turn the world right side up.") "So the word of the Lord grew and prevailed mightily" (Acts 19:20). The power of such meekness was revealed through Jesus, the good shepherd, then through his followers in his and their influence on the life of the world through succeeding centuries.[11]

The God of Justice

Central in the Bible is the idea of the God of justice. In an early event, Abraham, interceding for Sodom, poses this question to Yahweh, assuming the affirmative answer: "'Shall not the Judge of all the earth do right?'" (Genesis 18:25). Yahweh is seen as a God of justice in commands, descriptions, and events throughout the Pentateuch, as in "The Song of Moses" (Deuteronomy 32:4). Many Psalms also reflect that emphasis (e.g., 9:7-8; cf. 96:10-13). In the Prophets this motif comes to a new fullness: "For I the LORD love justice" (Isaiah 61:8). Amos (1 and 2) vividly portrays God's justice as a lion: All nations stand under the same kind of judgment. It acts as "a plumb line" for the conduct of life, even against Israel (7:7-9).

In the New Testament, the justice of God is assumed throughout, and sometimes explicitly expressed (Romans 3:26; 1 John 1:9; Revelation 15:3, reference to "The Song of Moses"). In general, the justice of God is caught up in a larger concept of the love of God, in that God metes out justice but through love gives grace, forgiveness, and constant new leases for larger life.

How justice is defined in the Bible is suggested by its being translated often in the King James Version as "judgment" or "righteousness," referring to the judgment or righteousness of God; in other words, justice is that which is "right" according to God's will. Jesus expressed this idea when he said, "My judgment is just; because I seek not mine own will, but the will of the Father which hath sent me" (John 5:30, KJV). God's will for justice is spelled out in specifics, such as God's oft expressed concern for the disadvantaged, the poor, the widows,

the orphans, the strangers. The concept of justice lays a heavy
emphasis on "social justice," as proclaimed by Amos, other
prophets, and Jesus.

Some question God's justice (Job, Malachi, some Psalms), but
through most of the Bible is the constant conviction: God is
just. His justice is not yet fully accomplished, but the will of
God and his Messiah is clear:

> ... he will make justice shine on every race
> never faltering, never breaking down,
> he will plant justice on the earth (Isaiah 42:4, *New English Bible*).

What response does this God of justice require of the believer?
To do justice. This means the believer must enter into human
relations which fulfill "social justice." It includes not oppressing
the poor, the widow, the orphan, the disadvantaged. Amos
spells this out in specifics, then speaks for God as not being
interested in animal sacrifices or certain rituals (5:21-24), but

> ... let justice roll down like waters,
> and righteousness like an everlasting stream.

Other prophets also call for justice:

> ... what does the LORD require of you
> but to do justice, and to love kindness,
> and to walk humbly with your God? (Micah 6:8).

Justice is to be institutionalized as well as personalized: "'These
are the things you should do: Speak the truth to one another.
In the courts give real justice—the kind that brings peace'"
(Zechariah 8:16, TEV; cf. Amos 5:15a). Note the relationship
of "justice" to "peace."

In the New Testament, Jesus emphasizes the divine imperative that believers do justice. We have already noted how
Jesus states his own mission as fulfillment of Isaiah's prophecy,
which emphasized justice (Luke 4:16-21). He tells the parable
of the rich man and the poor, sick beggar (Luke 16:19-31). In
the tradition of the prophets speaking out for justice, Jesus
gives this perspective on some religionists of his day: "'Woe to
you ... for you tithe mint and dill and cummin, and have
neglected the weightier matters of the law, justice and mercy
and faith; these you ought to have done, without neglecting
the others'" (Matthew 23:23). Jesus portrays the Final Judgment using as the criterion neither ritual nor theology, but

concern, or lack of it, for the hungry and thirsty, the stranger, the poor, the sick, the prisoner (Matthew 25:31-46).

The God who declares, "I hate ... injustice, and violence" (Zechariah 8:17, TEV) is the God who loves justice and peace. It is clear that the divine imperative is for the believer to do justice and to make peace.

The God of Freedom

One of the major themes in the Bible is freedom, seen as basic in the nature, works, and will of God.

A *leitmotif* in the Bible is God leading his people out of bondage in Egypt to freedom and "the promised land" (Exodus and parallel passages). This echoes throughout the Pentateuch, the books of history, Psalms, the Prophets and is reflected in the New Testament (Hebrews 11:23-29). It has been celebrated through the centuries in Jewish observances and in Christian remembrances of the Last Supper.

God is also reported in the Old Testament as repeatedly setting his people free. When they are unfaithful to him, he has them taken captive by other people, and when they repent, he frees them (Judges 3; 2; Chronicles 12; Psalms; the Prophets; Jeremiah 23).

In the New Testament, freedom under God is still important, but with new emphases. It is central to the mission of Jesus as he states it in his home synagogue in Nazareth, reading from Isaiah 61, emphasizing "release to the captives" and "to set at liberty those who are oppressed" (Luke 4:16-21). He teaches that his disciples shall know the truth, "and the truth will make you free" (John 8:31-32). He explains that they can be free from bondage to sin. He declares, ". . . if the Son makes you free, you will be free indeed" (John 8:36). Jesus brings freedom from the kinds of bondage cited in Isaiah and also freedom from prejudice, hatred, disease, and death.

Early Christians emphasized the freedom which God brought through his Messiah: "The law of the Spirit of life in Christ Jesus has set [us] free from the law of sin and death" (Romans 8:2). "For freedom Christ has set us free . . ." (Galatians 5:1). ". . . where the Spirit of the Lord is, there is freedom" (2 Corinthians 3:17). Paul writes that the whole creation "will be set free from its bondage to decay" and believers will "obtain the glorious liberty of the children of God" (Romans 8:19-21).

What is the response expected from the believer to the God of freedom? To guard freedom: "Stand fast therefore in the liberty wherewith Christ hath made us free" (Galatians 5:1, KJV, and much of the epistle, esp. chaps. 2; 3; 4; 5:13-14; 6:2, 9, 10; cf. Acts 15:10). Christians are to rejoice in the exercise of freedom. However, this is not a license to wanton living but liberty to live a new life through love to serve others (Galatians 5:13-14). They are to respect and be concerned for the freedom of others, but they are to go beyond that to loving others, bearing their burdens and serving them, thus bringing new freedom for all.

Some Conclusions

What can we conclude about the differing ideas about God in various parts of the Bible? Especially acute ·is the question of Yahweh, God of war. Can we today worship and obey the bloodbath commands of that wrathful God? Can we reconcile that war God with the God of life, peace, justice, freedom, the good shepherd, the God of love, as supremely revealed in Jesus Christ?

Such questions have a long lineage, some going back to the writers of the Old Testament, some to Jesus in his temptation and mission, some to the early Church Fathers and other Christians.

A simple answer was given by Marcion (second century) who urged the discard of the Old Testament with its bloody God.

However, the mainstream of church thinking rejected that. Much of Christian belief has its roots in the Old Testament; without it our New Testament and our faith would be difficult if not impossible to understand. But a problem remains for Christian education: Should the bloody parts of the Old Testament be used in teaching children? Teachers and church leaders should use discretion in choosing which age levels are able to deal with these difficult passages and the complex questions they raise. And if and when they are introduced, teachers should put them in balance, proportion, and perspective in interpreting them in relation to the rest of the Bible and life.

There is a Christian tradition which helps to reconcile the problem of the differing ideas about God and the question of the two Testaments. This is that "the New Testament is the

rule of faith and practice." Thus, the Old Testament is retained
and used for understanding, but the New Testament is seen
as containing what is basic to Christian faith and life.

On the specific problem of "Yahweh, God of war," scholars
have developed various views, such as the following: that this
was a primitive understanding of God, a concept held in common with ancient Israel's neighbors, with each people having
its own "warrior God." That in psycho-socio-religious development such ideas of God were outgrown in Bible times, as
demonstrated in other parts of Scripture. That by progressive
revelation God brought humankind to larger, clearer understanding of his real nature; in the New Testament the God of
love revealed himself to supplant the concepts of the God of
wrath and war in the Old Testament; God does care about
particular people, issues, and events which determine the course
of history, including wars; he was working out *heilsgeschichte*
("holy history"), the plan of salvation in the life of the world.
Again, this is an important large question, but one that goes
beyond the purview of this brief study. References for further
exploration are offered in the Notes, for example, notes 6 and
7.

In our survey we have seen that the concept of Yahweh as
a war God, pervasive as it is in part of the Old Testament, is
outweighed by the far larger number of, and much greater
emphasis upon, other ideas of God which move in the opposite
direction.

Further, we are aided by a basic understanding in herme-
neutics. It is widely accepted among Christian scholars and
lay people that the Bible is to be interpreted with "the mind
of Christ" insofar as we can discern it. This means that what
is in keeping with the life and teaching of Jesus and all of "the
Christ event" is to be considered as the revelation of God's
nature and will for us. If this principle is followed, we see
"Yahweh mighty in battle," and all the concomitant acts of
war waged in his name, not as revelation for us but as a
phenomenon of the beliefs and actions of the ancient Hebrews.
It is our understanding that God did not change *his nature*
from "the God of war" to "the God of peace." What happened
was that human understandings about God changed, especially, Christians believe, through God's revelation of his true
nature in Jesus Christ, the nonviolent "Suffering Servant"

Messiah, the Lord of love, and the Prince of Peace. In light of that revelation, the "war God" and the "holy war" concepts and actions are not operative for us in our faith and life. Rather, we think, believe, and act in the convictions which come to us through Jesus Christ and the corresponding truths in the Old and New Testaments. Thus, we live by the revelation and truth that God is a God of life, peace, justice, freedom, and love, caring for us as a good shepherd in all our problems and potentials as individuals and as God's whole human family.

Some verses in the Bible, apart from Yahweh passages, have been used as arguments for war—or against war by those who insist on interpreting passages in their context. Discussions of these could, and indeed do, constitute extensive studies. The reader who wishes to pursue this interest is referred to three important books dealing with such passages in detail, in the endnotes.[12] Here it must suffice to summarize that all these puzzling passages should be interpreted in the larger context of the nature of God, the peaceful messiahship which Jesus fulfilled, and the central hermeneutic principle of "the mind of Christ" as our basic guide to understanding the Scriptures.

Our second conclusion deals with the responses of believers which are to follow from the nature of God. In the Hebrew-Jewish-Christian tradition, believers are to seek to be and to act like the God they worship. The basis for the beliefs, the life, the conduct, and the ethics of the believer is the nature of God, who demands that his people be like him. There is an explicit statement of this principle in Leviticus 19:2: "'You shall be holy, for I, the LORD your God am holy.'" Jesus also invokes this principle repeatedly, as in Matthew 5:48.

Thus, as we have seen, the worshipers of Yahweh, who perceived him as a God of war, felt that they were to make war under his ensign, in his name.

However, based on our study of the nature of God in this chapter, we would emphasize the following:

As God is seen to be the God of life, we are to seek life more abundant for others and ourselves.

As God is seen to be the God of peace, we are to live in the spirit of peace and to be makers of peace.

As God is seen to be the good shepherd who is powerful and merciful, we are to be mighty and merciful, through meekness.

As God is seen to be the God of justice, we are to be just and
to do justice.

As God is seen to be the God of freedom, we are to be concerned about freedom for all, and to use it to serve others.

As God is seen to be the God of love, we are to be loving in
spirit and to live in ways of love.

How beautiful are the biblical visions of the nature of God,
of the Messiah, of God's reign of peace on earth! But sometimes
they seem so far from the cruel realities we see about us in
poverty, hunger, disease, hatred, prejudice, discrimination,
oppression, conflicts, terrors, the bloodbaths of recurring wars,
both large and small, and the awesome threat of thermonuclear
obliteration hanging over the human race. Amidst all this, the
believer is to live and work, faithful to God—to God's nature
and God's will for the lives of individuals and of the world—
knowing that God is working for peace, justice, freedom, and
a more abundant life for God's whole human family.

We are not to assume ultimate responsibilities for peace;
that rests with God. We are to be faithful in our thinking and
actions in accord with God's purposes for peace.

So what can we do more specifically? To that we address
ourselves in succeeding chapters.

What Do We Mean, "Peace"?

Love and fidelity have come together;
justice and peace join hands.
(Psalm 85:10, *New English Bible*)

W hy are you coming here to talk about peace? The Communists talk about peace! Why are you talking about peace?" This was more an exclamation than a question directed to a leader of a nationwide church program as he arrived at a state peace conference. He replied quietly, "Well, the Bible talks about peace. The Psalms and the Prophets, like Isaiah, speak of peace. Jesus was called 'the Prince of Peace.' And the New Testament reveals 'the God of peace.' So, on the basis of the Bible and our faith, we are concerned for peace. We should not let Communists take a monopoly on this idea so important to us as Christians." Then the speaker briefly cited differences between Communist and Christian ideas of peace; the Communists stress "order" and we stress "justice and freedom." The questioner expressed appreciation for the clarification and extended a more friendly welcome to the speaker for the conference on "peace."

"Peace" Has Many Meanings

"Peace" has been used to cover a multitude of meanings. Injustices have been done in the name of "peace." People have been oppressed "for peace." Wars have been fought "for peace."

A dramatic example of invoking "peace" to cover violence is found in Shakespeare's "Julius Caesar," Act 3, scene 1. After 55 the conspirators assassinate Caesar, his "friend," Brutus, says:

> . . . let us bathe our hands in Caesar's blood
> Up to the elbows, and besmear our swords;
> Then walk we forth, even to the market-place;
> And waving our red weapons o'er our heads,
> Let's all cry, "Peace, freedom, and liberty!"

For centuries, "peace" has been invoked by imperial powers around the world as a pretext to attack and rule others.

"Peace" as used by *leaders* in Communist-dominated areas, such as the Soviet Union, means "order" imposed by the constant threat or use of armed force upon their own and other peoples. Many Of *the people* in Communist-dominated lands hold a different view of peace. As we who have shared in fellowship and worship with people in the U.S.S.R. and other Communist-dominated countries can attest, many of them think of "peace" as friendship among peoples of the world, and as preventing war.

"Peace" can have such positive meanings as friendship, reconciliation, mutuality, and actions to avoid war. Or it can be used in camouflage, or in naivete, by those who cry "'Peace, peace,' when there is no peace" (Jeremiah 6:14).

It is imperative that when "we the people" are voting or undertaking other citizen responsibilities we be aware of how the term "peace" is being used, by various spokespersons. We should sharpen our skills in discerning shades of meaning, from the propagandistic to the profound, as "peace" is invoked by groups, movements, politicians, officials, and others.

Is Peace Personal?

Some people are primarily concerned about personal peace. They concentrate on peace within, peace of mind and spirit. That is important. Volumes have been and will be written about it.

For Jewish and Christian believers and many other religious adherents the ultimate source of such peace is God: "Thou wilt keep him in perfect peace, whose mind is stayed on thee: because he trusteth in thee" (Isaiah 26:3, KJV). The Hebrew idiom here for "perfect peace" is "peace, peace." Conversely, "There is no peace, saith the LORD, unto the wicked" (Isaiah 48:22, KJV).

While in this book our focus is international, we recognize a significant, two-way relationship between personal and world peace: Prophets, seers, and poets from Confucius to contemporaries have said that people at harmony within themselves can contribute better to harmony in widening circles, in the family, the community, the state, the nation, and the world. But also, peace in our environment can help us to find personal peace. This is seen in God's counsel: ". . . seek the peace of the city . . . for in the peace thereof shall ye have peace" (Jeremiah 29:7, KJV).

Keeping in mind the importance of personal peace, we focus in this book on the wider subject of peace in the world.

Is Peace Passive?

Peace is often thought of as quietness, calm, serenity, or even death. Standing by a quiet lake we think, "How peaceful . . . ." A hymn combines the personal and passive aspects of peace:

> Drop Thy still dews of quietness,
>   Till all our strivings cease;
> Take from our souls the strain and stress,
> And let our ordered lives confess
>   The beauty of Thy peace.[1]

In frontier days, the pioneer's struggles and labors done, he or she was placed in a grave marked by a wooden headstone with carved letters: R.I.P. Back of that hope, "Rest in Peace," lie centuries of Christian thought and liturgy.

In world affairs, some see peace as the absence of conflict, strife, or war, which is a somewhat passive perception. This accords with the Greek term *irene.* Surely peace does mean that, in part. But it also means much more. Peace*making* stresses active thinking and doing, creativity, imagination, development, and building. This accords with the Hebrew term *shalom.* We shall see such dynamics in defining "peace" and in ideas for seeking and pursuing it.

Peace and . . .?

Various thinkers have emphasized that peace is inherently related to other realities and values. We see this in the Bible:

> Love and fidelity have come together;
> justice and peace join hands.
> (Psalm 85:10, *New English Bible.*)

Many philosophers have related various virtues to peace. An example is Thomas Hobbes (1588–1679) who, in *Leviathan,* urged strong sovereign government because he saw the state of nature as a "war of every man against every man." He stressed *seeking peace* as a central law of nature with other laws related. He saw "justice," "mercy," and a dozen other "natural laws" as instrumental to bringing peace. As every person's self-interest is best served by peace, people, with fears and desires leading them to hope for something better, will employ reason and discover these precepts or "natural laws" which make for peace.[2]

Peace and/or Order?

"Order" or "world order" is often used as a synonym for "peace." What are the meanings and relationships of these terms?

Two concepts of social order are at opposite ends of a continuum: at one pole, order is forced by outward compulsion; at the other, it is developed from inward impulsion of people.

The one extreme is utilized by rulers in the U.S.S.R. and other Communist-dominated lands. They say "peace" to describe the "order" which is imposed by military force or its continuous threat, and by psychological, political, and economic pressures.

A cardinal doctrine in Marxism was: all nations in Communist control are in "peace." That doctrine was smashed by these events: the Yugoslavian and Albanian splits from Moscow; the Soviets' military aggression to crush struggles for freedom in Hungary and Czechoslovakia; their re-oppressing East German and Polish people by multiple pressures; the brutal invasion of Afghanistan by the U.S.S.R. to destroy one Marxist puppet to set up another; the Sino-Soviet split; and other economic, political, and ideological conflicts among different Marxist regimes.

"Peace," as used by Communist rulers, means that "order" may be imposed by more powerful nations on weaker ones to crush out justice, freedom, and human rights in the name of "peace."

At the other pole, "peace" or "order" is voluntary cooperation within and among nations. The Great Seal of the U.S.A. bears, within and among nations. The Great Seal of the U.S.A. bears, on the reverse side, words of an ancient thinker, Virgil, "*NOVUS ORDO SECLORUM*" *(a new order of the ages),* and an unfinished pyramid, meaning there is more order to be built. (See a dollar bill, reverse side.) This expressed the hope of the founders of the U.S.A. for voluntary cooperation at home and among the nations.

Internationally, an impressive illustration of such "order" is the world's longest unfortified border, that between Canada and the United States. A "new order" is seen also in regional organizations in the European Community, in the Americas, Africa, and Asia.

The UN is based on voluntary cooperation and democracy. These are part of its present strength and weakness. We shall consider its roles, problems, achievements, and potentials in a later chapter. Suffice it to note here that it embodies beginnings of world order and underscores the urgent need to utilize ideas, relationships, and structures to develop a voluntary "world order" which will bring more assurance of real peace.

Peace and/or Justice?

"Peace" *or* "justice"? Goethe, among others, posed this question as a moral dilemma. Persons in the 1940s found themselves faced with such a dilemma when confronted by Hitler's Nazism. Reinhold Niebuhr and others, in the U.S.A., held that "peace" must yield to "justice."[3] They abjured "peace" in the short run to hope for it in the long run. So they supported war to defeat Nazism because of its injustice, mass murders, and threats of more outrages on other peoples. On the other hand, A. J. Muste and pacifists made the opposite case: That widening the war would increase injustice in the world, and that as much peace as possible should be kept.[4]

"Peace *with* justice and freedom" was stressed for postwar planning in the 1940s by the Federal Council of Churches through its Commission on a Just and Durable Peace. With the statesmanship of its leaders, Executive Director Walter W. Van Kirk and Chairman John Foster Dulles, it stressed that if postwar peace were to endure, it would have to be built on justice. Others shared in the growing use of the idea of "a just and durable peace."

In considering "justice," as with "peace," it is imperative that we discern clearly the meaning intended by various users. Recently, "justice" was called for in the Middle East by Egypt's President Mubarak, Syrian President al-Assad, Israel's Prime Minister Begin, P.L.O. leaders, the late Soviet President Brezhnev, U.S. officials, and others. "Justice" and "a just peace" would have widely different meanings to them all. So it is important for us to define "justice" as we are using it.

Let us start with the popular idea of "justice" as summarized in ancient times by the Latin phrase, *suum cuique*, "to each his own." But it is so difficult to discern what is "just" for each and all, that prophets, theologians, philosophers, statesmen, and others have struggled through the centuries to define its meaning.

In general in the Bible, as we have seen, "justice" was understood as "righteousness," or "rightness," according to the will of God. In a classic statement putting the two in parallel, the prophet Amos declared that this is God's will:

" . . . let justice roll down like waters,
    and righteousness like an everflowing stream" (Amos 5:24).

We see further dimensions of "justice" in God's oft expressed concern for the disadvantaged, the poor, the widows, the orphans, and the strangers.

Among the philosophers, Aristotle is much quoted as he pioneered in exploring the meaning of "justice." He stressed "distributive justice" on the basis of merit and "corrective justice" for rectifying errors which exist in distribution.

In our time, a theologian, Tillich, wrote ontologically of three levels of justice.[5] First is "a claim raised silently or vocally by a being on the basis of its power of being." Second, echoing Aristotle, Tillich cites "tributive or proportional justice." This appears as "distributive, attributive, retributive justice, giving to everything proportionally to what it deserves, positively or negatively." Third, he proposes "transforming or creative justice," expressed in "fulfillment within the unity of universal fulfillment. The religious symbol for this is the kingdom of God." In sum, "Justice in its ultimate meaning is creative justice, and creative justice is the form of reuniting love."

Major work on "justice" has been done by a contemporary philosopher, John Rawls.[6] He presents "a conception of justice which generalizes and carries to a higher level of abstraction the familiar theory of the social contract as found, say, in Locke, Rousseau, and Kant." He proposes two principles:

> First: each person is to have an equal right to the most extensive basic liberty compatible with a similar liberty for others.
> Second: social and economic inequalities are to be arranged so they are both (a) reasonably expected to be to everyone's advantage, and (b) attached to positions and offices open to all.

Rawls's thinking is particularly relevant to current use of the word "justice" in international affairs since it does not denote rewards and punishment but more equity in economic and social terms.

"Justice" is no mere abstraction. It signifies struggling to find out and to practice what is fair and equitable in economic, political, and social realities, and all aspects of life. It is not charity. It involves new shaping of the economic, political, and social structures and operations in the U.S.A. and around the world to make for "justice for all."

Unless there is relative "justice," there can be no lasting "peace." And unless there is "peace," "justice" is largely destroyed. Wars wreak havoc on "justice." Wars have not usually confirmed who is right, but who is left when the killing ends. Those who have won wars have generally been those who had the strongest or most effectively used military force. In moral reality, "might does *not* make right." Wars have brought many of history's most massive injustices to nations and to countless millions of people in their individual lives—or deaths.

Such integral relationships between "peace" and "justice" mean that it is impossible, in the long run, to have one without the other. They are interdependent and can be mutually reinforcing. So, while at times we may be faced with the dilemma of "peace" *or* "justice," more generally we must work toward "peace" *and* "justice." To have "peace," we must build a more "just" social order; to have "justice," we must create a more "peaceful" social order. So, in this book we use "peace" as inextricably bound with "justice."

Peace and/or Freedom

"Freedom" was a basic concern in the 1940s. "The Four Freedoms" were set forth by President Roosevelt in his State of the Union Message, January 6, 1941: Freedom of Speech,

Freedom of Religion, Freedom from Want, Freedom from Fear. He and Churchill dealt with "freedoms" in the Atlantic Charter, 1941. The U.S.A., the U.K., and the U.S.S.R. emphasized "freedom" in the United Nations Declaration, January 1, 1942. Other leaders in public life, churches, synagogues, and NGOs stressed "freedom" in relation to "peace" during the 1940s and 1950s.

Around the world the tides of "freedom" flowed strongly. In Asia, India's independence in 1947 led the way as scores of colonies became "free." In Africa, the cry *"Uhuru!"* ("Freedom!") rang with effectiveness. So many of its new nations entered the UN in 1960 that it was called "the African year." The old, imposed "order" of colonialism ended, except for a few important vestiges, as in southern Africa. The UN made a major contribution in helping the process to be mostly peaceful.

During three "Decades of Development" in the 1960s, 1970s, and now the 1980s, over one hundred less developed nations have been seeking "a new economic order" with more "justice" to make their "freedom" more real in economic terms and more fruitful in the lives of their people. In Latin America, especially, the struggle continues for *economic* "freedom." More subtle and complex than political independence, this is not solved by signing a document and running up a new flag. Economic "freedom" around the globe is one of the most urgent items of unfinished business on the world's agenda.

A worldwide survey revealed that 1981 "has not been a good year for freedom."[7] In its tenth annual comparative survey, Freedom House reports the following: Slightly over one-third of the world's people, about 36 percent (in 54 nations and 27 related territories) live in generally "free" situations; 20 percent (in 49 countries and 23 territories) live in "partly free" situations; 44 percent (in 52 countries and 4 territories) live in areas characterized as "not free." A significant factor in those "not free" areas is the Communist takeover of various countries in the aftermath of World War II in Eastern Europe, and more recently in Asia. Such countries have moved in differing degrees from an earlier monolithic pattern of oppression, but most remain at least highly authoritarian with severe repression of people.

Decreases of democracy and increases of dictatorship and authoritarianism have been hailed by Communist ideologues as "the wave of the future." It seems some would welcome the universalization of the nightmare of Orwell's *1984* with life under "big brother"—if they are "big brother." But such trends since 1945 can be seen as backwashes in the stream of history.

Some developments during recent decades show gains for "freedom." For instance, although many newer nations have retreated from the democracy of their early independence to more authoritarian rule (for the time being only, it is to be hoped), there is more "freedom" around the world in the last thirty-five years because of the breaking of the bonds of colonialism. Also, as these nations make economic and social progress, there is promise they will be able to develop more democracy and "freedom." In the Communist-dominated countries there have been increasing and significant stirrings of the human spirit for more freedom. Dissent is growing in remarkable ways in the U.S.S.R. and its satellites in movements for more "freedom," for example, Solidarity in Poland.

"The trends run toward freedom" was the conclusion of an editorial titled "Since Budapest," written about such developments. It was evoked by events in Poland and the concurrent twenty-fifth anniversary of the Hungarian revolt for freedom.

> . . . Hungary found a more devious path toward a more humane form of dictatorship. Rumania wriggled free of many Soviet economic and diplomatic restraints. East Germany acquiesces in tight rule but has gradually tolerated more civilized ties with West Germany. And Poland, always seething with dissent and anti-Soviet feeling, has now invented an entirely new kind of challenge, all the more alarming to the Kremlin because it is throwing up leaders outside the Communist fold.
>
> Nationalisms are sprouting also in Western Europe, but they are no kinder to Communists. East and West, the trends run toward freedom.[8]

Our reading of history can lead us to the view that the future may be seen as offering not less but more freedom. In *The Promise of the Coming Dark Age,* L. S. Stavrianos develops the theme that human advances in history can be seen in the larger liberties attained by the masses of mankind in succeeding periods.[9] Some of us anticipate that beyond the present "backwash" of dictatorships and authoritarian regimes the tide of history will move toward more democracy and "freedom" around the planet. Such hope can motivate us to redouble our efforts to seek "peace with freedom."

The impact of "peace" upon "freedom" is significant and positive; that of "war" is insidious and negative. In peaceful environments, usually, there is more freedom. In a state of war, or even a situation of fear of armed conflict, one of the first victims is "freedom." The deeper the crisis, the worse is the curtailment of "freedom." So, if we have a concern for "freedom," we should be motivated all the more to work against the institution of war—and to seek peace.

"Peace with justice and freedom" has been a persistent theme in U.S. foreign policy since World War II. When Dulles was secretary of state, he constantly stressed, as he had done in leadership in the Federal Council of Churches' Commission on a Just and Durable Peace, the integral relationships of "peace, justice, and freedom."

Some depreciation of the word "freedom" came during the "Cold War" when it was loosely used. Many who employed the term "the free world" included in it the dictatorial, military governments then in power in Spain, Portugal, and other lands. So the terms "free" and "freedom" became tarnished. However, the stress on "freedom" as related to "peace" persists in U.S. foreign policy at least in rhetoric, if not always in practice.

Part of the reason for "freedom" being an important attribute of "peace" is that it is inherently significant for the meaning of life both for groups and for individuals. In the Hebrew-Jewish-Christian tradition, "freedom" is a meaningful motif. As we saw in the chapter on the Bible, persistent in the Old Testament is the concept of God's leading his people from captivity to "freedom," as in the exodus from slavery in Egypt to independence in the Promised Land. In the New Testament is the thought of "the glorious liberty of the children of God" (Romans 8:21). Such ideas have contributed to wider concerns for freedom for groups and persons in the world.

While the emphasis on freedom in the New Testament often concentrates on liberty from the old law and sin and death, there are also broader emphases, which have been applied to freedom in political and social life. Attest the impact of Luther, Roger Williams, and others. Christian ideas have remarkably influenced Western political thought, in relation to rights and freedom, as seen in the thinking of Locke (much influenced by the theologian Hooker), Mill, Kant, and others. Their influence can be traced through the Declaration of Independence, the

Constitution of the U.S.A., and a whole range of developments for freedom and human rights, including the Universal Declaration of Human Rights; the International Covenants on Civil and Political Rights, and on Economic, Social and Cultural Rights; and other documents and operations of the UN system and of many nations.

"Freedom" has real significance in terms of what it means to be human. For the philosopher Rousseau, "moral liberty was not simply, as for Locke, a right that persons have; it was a person's very humanity, what makes him human."[10] Contemporary reassertions of such ideas are made by thinkers like Noam Chomsky. He challenges the "behaviorists" for their rigidities and lack of comprehensive understanding of what it means to be human. He holds that in human beings there is an innate need for freedom, for the rights to question and explore.[11]

Like "justice," "freedom" as we are using it is no mere abstraction. We are concerned for its concrete forms: personal, political, economic, social, cultural, and religious. We envision "freedom" for all persons and groups to exercise their human rights and seek to realize their highest potentials. Thus, freedom is "freedom to become," to become human, in all its fullest senses. That leads us to the subject of "humanization" in our next section.

Peace and Humanization

The power of "an idea whose time has come"[12] may be in the concept of "humanization." A new chapter of the history of peace is being written in the increasing concerns around the globe for human values, human rights, and human development.

Through the ages some saints, philosophers, and statesmen have had basic concerns for human beings. In the Bible we have seen divine and human caring about persons. In classical Greece, art, drama, literature, and philosophy evidenced appreciation of and concern for what it means to be human. Plato and Aristotle taught that government should enrich the lives of the people in truth, beauty, goodness, and the eternal. Their human caring was stressed by a modern Greek, Doxiadis, who also sought better cities for human life: "The ultimate goal of *Anthropos* (the human being) as Aristotle defined it, 'is to be happy and safe in his city and to have his *polis* (government) assist in his human development.'"[13] Some Romans cared for humanity as seen in the saying of Terence: *"Homo sum; humani nil a me alienum puto."*[14] Others, sharing the view that they were human and therefore counting nothing human to be indifferent to them, included Epictetus, Cicero, and Augustine with his concern for people and a new "City of God."

In succeeding centuries some religious leaders, theologians, philosophers, artists, scientists, statesmen, and others have had basic concerns for human values. Witness the variety ranging from St. Francis of Assisi, through Erasmus, Charles Dickens, Abraham Lincoln, Jane Addams, Albert Schweitzer, Toyohiko Kagawa, Mahatma Gandhi, Albert Einstein, George Washington Carver, Mother Teresa, Danny Kaye, and Martin Luther King, Jr.

Concerns for human rights and values were expressed by some political philosophers. Hume suggested that we approve certain more important virtues, "such as justice and benevolence, because they promote the interest of humanity."[15] Locke emphasized "human rights" including "the right of persons to govern themselves" and "life, liberty, or possessions."[16] These were related to his vision for a better world as "one community or society of all humanity."[17] His influence is clear in the Declaration of Independence and the Constitution of the U.S.A.

Growing from the thinking and acting on human concerns through centuries, there is now on a world scale the early flowering of "humanization." The emerging of planetary, comprehensive concern for human rights, human values, and human development is seen in the development of the UN Charter, the Universal Declaration of Human Rights, and International Covenants on Civil and Political Rights and on Economic, Social and Cultural Rights. The U.S.A. abdicated its world leadership for human rights by withdrawing from the Covenant drafting because of the Bricker Amendment threat and racism, in 1953, causing an ebb tide. But other nations took courage and persevered. The intrepid, prescient UN Secretary-General, Dag Hammarskjöld, set forth the issues of rights and peace:

... the question of peace and the question of human rights are closely related. Without recognition of human rights we shall never have peace, and it is only within the framework of peace that human rights can be fully developed.[18]

With his courageous leadership for human rights and peace, and with the cooperation of colleagues, such concerns became more dynamic in the thinking, structures, and programs of the UN. Declarations to advance human rights opposed discrimination and set forth rights for women, children, youth, the handicapped, and, indeed, all human beings.[19]

Principles from the Universal Declaration and drafting of the International Covenants were written into the constitutions of many of the more than one hundred new nations. Even though human rights may not be fully observed yet, it is basic to have them recognized and set forth in declarations, covenants, constitutions, and laws as steps in their realization.

During the 1970s international activities demonstrated an increase in the concern for human rights. In addition to the continuing work of the UN Commission on Human Rights, including the annual report of achievements and failures around the world, the UN took special actions: in 1973, the General Assembly's proclamation of a "Decade for Action to Combat Racism and Racial Discrimination"; a World Conference for Action Against *Apartheid,* in Lagos, Nigeria, in 1977; a World Conference to Combat Racism and Racial Discrimination, in Geneva in 1978.

Once, many perceived human rights in a somewhat negative, narrower sense, that is, that persons were not to be deprived of political participation and concomitant conditions; now, it is seen that human rights comprise the quality of life including relations and resources to help people realize their human potential.

These rights range from the most basic to the higher levels. "Human rights begin in the stomach."[20] With illumination from fields of psychology and administration, as in Maslow's "hierarchy of needs,"[21] we are aware that people need basic resources for survival and security, such as food, pure water, shelter, and employment; but persons also require social, psychological, aesthetic, and spiritual opportunities for human self-fulfillment.

Such twentieth-century concerns accord with some of those of Christianity. Jesus stated about his mission to people: "I am come that they might have life, and that they might have it more abundantly" (John 10:10, KJV).

In our time, a Christian theologian, Paul Lehmann, writing

extensively about God's work in the world, says, in sum: "What God is doing in the world to make and to keep life human is to bring about human maturity; in other words, to bring to pass a new humanity."[22]

Other Christians in the World Council of Churches succinctly summarized some of the goals for a more just world: ". . . human freedom and fulfillment."[23]

The conditions for "life more abundant," "human maturity," and "human fulfillment" in our world include the "resources to become" (justice), "the liberty to become" (freedom), and the "rights to become" more fully human (humanization).

It is difficult to find one word to summarize all those realities, to carry all the meanings we have in mind. A relevant term was used by Teilhard de Chardin: "Hominization."[24] We seek something less abstract and more personal than the ideas he expounded under that Latinized term. So we use the word "humanization." In defining it, we go beyond dictionary definitions. We include *a concern for human values, human rights, and human development, expressed in thinking and acting to help people as individuals, as groups, and as our whole species, to grow as fully as possible toward their maximum potentials.*

Our concept carries no coercion. In "humanization" there is *no* imposing it on other persons or groups as has sometimes been done with "civilization"! Also, it means the opposite of "dehumanization" as in colonial, imperialistic, authoritarian, dictatorial, or totalitarian regimes, or as in some instances in capitalist systems. It emphasizes "humanity" in relationships as opposed to "man's inhumanity to man." It means sharing relationships and resources which will help individuals and groups to develop their fullest potentials according to what *they* understand it means to be "human." "Humanization" means having respect for each individual, for the dignity of persons and groups. It means dealing with others not as "things" but as other "humans," thinking and acting in human relations not as "I-it" but as "I-Thou."[25]

"Humanization" means going beyond "live and let live" to "live and help live."[26] Here is life more abundant for others—and for ourselves, because it is mutual.

"Humanization" is no mere abstraction; it means providing specifics such as food, jobs, housing, education, and health; natural resources and energy availability; a beneficent biosphere; and development of the arts, sciences, and technology for human growth.

In relation to "peace," we may see "humanization" as ways in which our race is moving, slowly, sometimes two steps forward, one step back, from a world of war toward one of peace. When we respect other human beings, when we gain more "reverence for life," when we, as persons and nations, relate to others with *basic* concern for human values, the institution of war will be discarded as unacceptable in human international relations. Other, more human ways of working at our problems in this small, interdependent society on "Spaceship Earth" are being developed: for example, "conflict resolution" and international organization. However, all need to be expedited much faster and farther.

As a conceptual framework for such a vision of the coming world of peace, we can picture the spasmodic development of humanity through many stages constituting three basic levels:

1. "Barbarianism," with its ages-long and still widely accepted pattern of "kill and be killed," "man's inhumanity to man," and "world wars."

2. "Civilization," with its ameliorizing adjustments toward a pattern of "live and let live," growing toleration, and attempts at "balances of power" and "coexistence," hoping to postpone or stave off wars.

3. "Humanization," with its pattern of "live and help live," mutuality, "love" on a planetary scale, all leading to an emerging world of "peace."

"Peace" with "Justice," "Freedom"—and "Humanization"

We use the concept of "humanization" to complement and augment "justice" and "freedom." As we have seen, one imperative for "peace" is "justice." However, justice is often interpreted in such a narrow sense as not to be seasoned by mercy. We have seen that another imperative for "peace" is "freedom." But it is interpreted in ambiguous ways. To clarify those concepts and bring added substance to them and to the meaning of "peace," we propose using "humanization" to complement "justice" with compassion and "freedom" with responsibility. "Humanization" comprises concerns not only for equity and liberty but also for helping to provide incentives and resources to enable individuals to develop their fullest potentials.

The relationships among "order," "justice," "freedom," and "humanization" can be synergistic and mutually reinforcing. However, these realities are often in conflict, or at least in tension of varying degrees. Extreme emphasis upon one can be destructive of others. "Order" can be imposed at the expense of "justice," "freedom," and "humanization." "Justice" can be claimed as a reason for destroying "order," "freedom," and "humanization." "Freedom" can be sought in ways that can disrupt "order," "justice," and "humanization." Therefore, putting these values into practice demands constant sensitivity and care by us and all decision makers to keep them in balance and, in Reinhold Niebuhr's phrase, in "creative tension."

In working through decisions, often dealing with cruel dilemmas, "humanization" might well serve as a reference point for the other realities and values. This focus was set by the poet Edwin Markham: "Why build these cities glorious if man unbuilded goes?"[27] Now, in "humanization" we have the opportunity for contemporary application of the ancient counsel, "Man is the measure of all things,"[28] or as we would update it, "Human beings are the measure of all things." As Christians, we understand this to be in God's will for all of humanity.

"Peace"

"Peace," then, as we are using this term, with light from the Bible, Christian tradition, theologians, philosophers, statesmen, and political scientists, is integrally related to "justice," to "freedom," to "humanization"—and to "love" as seen in our next chapter.

Throughout this book we shall generally use the word "peace" by itself. However, that is to be understood usually as being shorthand for the whole interrelated constellation of concepts including "order," "justice," "freedom," "humanization," and "love."

4

Love and Peace?

> ". . . love the Lord your God . . .
> and love your neighbor as yourself. . . ."
> (Matthew 22:37-39)

"Love," based on biblical understanding, can have remarkable influence on international relations for "peace." One illustration is the way Christians in the U.S.A. and in the U.S.S.R. pioneered in breaking down the "iron curtain" separating two large parts of the human race, those in the "Western world" and those in the Soviet Union and its satellites. Christians in the National Council of the Churches of Christ in the U.S.A. and in various churches in the U.S.S.R., including the Russian Orthodox and the Baptist and Evangelical churches, believing they were led by the Spirit of the God of love, took this venture of faith in 1955 and years following. They acted on the basis of biblical conviction that Jesus Christ "is our peace, who hath made both one, and hath broken down the middle wall of partition [iron curtain] between us" (Ephesians 2:14, KJV) and that "God . . . hath given to us the ministry of reconciliation" (2 Corinthians 5:18, KJV). After much thought, prayer, and careful preparation, these groups of Christians carried out a series of international exchanges to the U.S.S.R. and to the U.S.A. The exchanges resulted in new understandings, attitudes, and relationships among Christians and others whom they influenced and were instrumental in starting ero-

sion of the political and psychological "iron curtain." This opened
the way to improving international relations.

"Love" in the Hebrew-Jewish Tradition

We have seen, in the chapter on the Bible, that ideas such
as "lovingkindness" and "tender mercies" used to describe God
who is a God of "love" are found in the Old Testament. Amid
a pervasive emphasis on fear, significant is God's love for his
people; this is a basic assumption in the Hebrew-Jewish tradition. (See the Pentateuch, historical books, Psalms, the
Prophets, especially Hosea, Jeremiah, Ezekiel.)

The second dimension of "love," the believer's love of God,
is seen through the Old Testament, epitomized in Deuteronomy
6:4-5; 7:6-11; 10:12-13; 10:17–11:1, combining fear and love
toward God.

The third dimension of "love," the believer's love of others,
is also seen in the Old Testament, as in Leviticus 19:15-18,
which sets forth laws for relations with others, including "love
your neighbor."

Two differing lines of thought persist in the Old Testament
regarding "love your neighbor." One is exclusive, confining the
duty to fellow Israelites (and resident strangers). The other is
inclusive, emphasizing that God is the LORD of all creation,
and that while he has a special love for Israel, he loves all
peoples (e.g., Amos 9:7). Thus, the believer's duty to "love your
neighbor" is universalized. We see this in some of the Prophets.
In Isaiah the moving "Suffering Servant Songs" reveal that
God's people are chosen not for self-gratification but for service
to the world. Their suffering would bring redemption for others
and restoration for themselves (e.g., 40, 42, 49, 66).

Other Old Testament books, such as Ruth and Jonah, carry
the inclusive view. Many people miss the major message of
Jonah because they get so hooked on the fish story that they
miss the point of it all, which is the broader love of God for
other people, which the believers should also have.

The Portrait of "Love" in Jesus' Ministry

"Love" is defined in the New Testament by the nature of God
revealed in the incarnation in Jesus Christ (e.g., John 3:16; 2
Corinthians 5:19; 1 John 4:8-9). We see God's love in Jesus
from Christmas to Calvary to "the contemporary Christ." The

world's best portrait of love is in "the Christ event": Jesus' birth, growth, life, teaching, ministries, passion, resurrection, glorification, and what he still does in the lives of people and in the world.

"Love" is at the center of his ministry. Jesus goes about giving himself away, to meet others' needs. In "the Galilean springtime" of his ministry, he is teaching, preaching, healing, and otherwise helping people (Matthew 4:23; Luke 7:19 ff.). The acts of Jesus are not destructive but constructive and creative. His passion and sacrifice energize his disciples in succeeding centuries as the supreme symbol of self-giving love.

The Great Commandment

Jesus is asked by one skilled in the law a favorite question of that time: "Which is the great commandment in the law?" Jesus gives a succinct reply to him—and to history: "'You shall love the Lord your God ... and You shall love your neighbor as yourself. On these two commandments depend all the law and the prophets'" (Matthew 22:37-40; cf. Mark 12:28-34; Luke 10:25-37). That last sentence is also of great significance. Jesus takes two ideas from the Old Testament and makes them essential in religion. We saw them in Deuteronomy 6:4-5 (cf. 10:12-13) and Leviticus 19:18. Jesus selects these two sentences, which could easily be missed among the Scripture's hundreds of laws and thousands of verses. He combines them; thus they "have had an incalculable influence on Western culture"[1] and they hold greater potential for life and peace in the world.

The exclusive or inclusive view of "love thy neighbor" is still being debated in Jesus' time (Luke 10:25-37). The one skilled in the law asks Jesus, "And who is my neighbor?" Luke says he was trying "to justify himself,"—possibly defending his narrow view. In reply, Jesus tells the parable of "the good Samaritan." The hostility between the Jews and the Samaritans makes it most meaningful that Jesus chooses for the hero not a Jew but one of the hated Samaritans. He is "the neighbor" to whom love is due! Jesus takes the inclusive, universal view.

Jesus' Teaching About "Love"

Jesus sums up "the Good News" in another central, most quoted verse, John 3:16. God's love is put at the heart of reli-

gion. In saying "God so loved the world" (or "all people"), Jesus
pushes the meaning of "love" beyond any narrow bounds to
the universal. He sets forth specifics in his "Sermon on the
Mount." Most striking is his counsel to love even enemies!
(Matthew 5:43-48). Note the basic motive for such unusual
love: the nature of God. Again contradicting centuries of common wisdom (which some still hold), Jesus sets aside the *lex
talionis* and puts in its place "turning the other cheek" (Matthew 5:38-39). How revolutionary in the history of human
relations! A further specific probably does not sit well with
many hearers who had been commandeered by Roman occu-
pation soldiers: "And whosoever shall compel thee to go a mile,
go with him twain" (Matthew 5:41, KJV). "Going the second
mile" is often used to mean simply going beyond one's duty.
But Jesus' counsel applies to relations with those considered
"enemies." Carrying their heavy gear for a second mile, beyond
the required one, could warmly surprise the occupiers and open
better relations.

In the Beatitudes, starting the "Sermon on the Mount" (5:5),
Jesus says, "'Blessed are the meek: for they shall inherit the
earth.'" We saw the roots of this in the Psalms (37:11) and the
Prophets conveying tremendous, quiet power. "'Blessed are the
merciful: for they shall obtain mercy,'" is self-explanatory for
"love." Then comes: "'Blessed are the peacemakers: for they
shall be called the children of God.'" (Matthew 5:9, KJV). Much
of the world's conventional emotion calls them otherwise: Cursed
are the yellow-bellies who will not support war; for they shall
be called traitors. But the statement of Jesus carries the weight
of understanding the nature of God. A more specific rendering
of the Greek here intensifies the insight: "they shall be ac-
knowledged as the children of God."[2] Those who believe in God
will realize that peacemakers are partaking of the very nature
and activity of God.

Such terms as "peacemakers" and "love" can apply not only
to pacifists but also to all who are dedicated to working for
peace.

"The Sermon on the Plain" (Luke 6:20-49) reinforces and
gives added nuances to "love" as seen in "The Sermon on the
Mount" (see esp. vv. 27-38). The rest of Jesus' teaching is also
filled by the spirit of "love," giving one's self to meet others'
needs.

The parable of the prodigal son, or better, of the forgiving Father, depicts God's love which understands, reaches out, reconciles, and brings new relationships (Luke 15:11-32).

The parable of the ninety and nine, or better, of the seeking shepherd, also demonstrates God's love reaching out to find, rescue, and restore one lost sheep (Luke 15:3-7).

Other teaching portrays what it means to lack love: a rich man living in luxury, ignoring the hunger and sickness of Lazarus begging by his gate, at his own peril (Luke 16:19-31); a rich young ruler declining Jesus' counsel to give his wealth to the poor and follow him, at the cost of the kingdom of God (18:18-25).

Dramatically, Jesus pictures the Final Judgment. Its basis is not theological orthodoxy nor group membership but justice, as we have seen, and whether people act in love for the needy (Matthew 25:31-46).

Against self-aggrandizement and domination over others, Jesus sets the new way of self-giving love. When the disciples dispute as to which should be greatest, he says, "'If any one would be first, he must be last of all and servant of all'" (Mark 9:35). Jesus stresses the same to a multitude: "'He who is greatest among you shall be your servant'" (Matthew 23:11). When James and John ask if they can sit on either side of him in glory, Jesus shares with all his disciples the idea that against the world's way of dominating others, they are to live out love in self-giving service. Whoever would be great should minister; and whoever would be chief, should be servant of all. "For even the Son of man came not to be ministered unto, but to minister, and to give his life a ransom for many" (Mark 10:42-45, KJV, and parallel passages).

Zacchaeus, a short, rich tax collector, climbs a tree to see Jesus, who invites himself to lunch. Zacchaeus comes down and takes Jesus to his house. There he responds to the Lord of love, and he finds a new spirit of love within himself, "Behold, Lord, the half of my goods I give to the poor; and if I have taken any thing from any man by false accusation, I restore him fourfold" (Luke 19:1-10, KJV). Jesus declares, "This day is salvation come to this house."

At "The Last Supper" Jesus gives "a new commandment": ". . . love one another; as I have loved you . . ." (John 13:34-35, KJV).

In Jesus' teaching about "love" there is a paradox: in giving one's self away to God and the needs of others, one finds one's self and life abundant and eternal (Luke 9:23-25, and parallel passages).

"Love" as Understood by Earlier and Later Disciples

What happened to the idea of "love" after the life and teaching of Jesus? Among his early followers, "love" continued to be a central theme. All New Testament writers reinforced the concept of "love" as set forth by Jesus in John 3:16. The response they called for echoes the Great Commandment: Believers are to love God and others. "God is love"; therefore, love God, keep his commandments, and love others. That is the Johannine letters' summary.

Most of the New Testament writers contain a didactic or hortatory element, spelling out the praxis of "love." Paul, with the concept of "faith working through love" (Galatians 5:6b), sets forth specifics of "the more excellent way" of "love" in 1 Corinthians 12:31–14:1. Again, in Romans 12 he spells out practical meanings of "love" including, as we noted in chapter 2, references to "peace." Far from being soft and sentimental, "love," as Paul sees it, is the mightiest force in the universe! (Romans 8, esp. vv. 31-39).

"Love" coming from God is a reconciling force: "And all things are of God, who hath reconciled us to himself by Jesus Christ, and hath given to us the ministry of reconciliation." In this we are "ambassadors for Christ" (2 Corinthians 5:18-20, KJV).

"Reconciliation" is emphasized in a cosmic account of salvation as the believers, instead of "having no hope, and without God in the world," now have "peace" and new relationships.

> For he is our peace, who hath made both one, and hath broken down the middle wall of partition between us . . . so making peace; and that he might reconcile both unto God . . . and came and preached peace to you which were afar off, and to them that were nigh. . . . Now therefore ye are no more strangers and foreigners, but fellowcitizens with the saints, and of the household of God (Ephesians 2:14-19, KJV).

"Reconciliation" is stressed also in Colossians in a cosmic setting for the work and grace of God. Again, practical results are seen: now "there is neither Greek nor Jew . . . Barbarian, Scythian, bond nor free. . . ." Other practical results are that "the new person" in Christ has put off, among other things, "anger, wrath, malice" (Colossians 3:8-11, KJV).

The praxis of "love" is also spelled out in specific terms in 1 Peter 3:8-11, in the exhortation cited in the chapter on the Bible; it ends with the phrase from Psalm 34:14 used for our title, "seek peace and pursue it."

In the Johannine letters, the praxis of "love" includes four major points relevant to our purposes: having compassion for and sharing our possessions with those in need (1 John 3:17-18); providing Christian hospitality to fellow-believers and to strangers (3 John 5-8); loving not the world and its evils (1 John 2:15-17); not hating, but loving others (1 John 2:9-11; 3:10-15).

Differing emphases on "loving the neighbor" are found in various parts of the New Testament. One is "love" to fellow-Christians (Petrine and Johannine letters). The wider focus (Jesus, Paul, Ephesians, Colossians) envisions the love by God and by believers in universal, even cosmic, dimensions.

Through the centuries, countless Christians have composed a library on "love," which we cannot survey here. We note, however, in the past fifty years a new, significant concern among Christians on the subject of "love."

At the forefront of this new concern about love was the extensive analysis by Anders Nygren, *The Christian Idea of Love,* in Swedish, 1932; this was translated into English, in 1937–1939 and was titled *Agape and Eros.*[3] In this work he compares New Testament thought with Greek philosophy: *Agape* is *the* fundamental and central idea of the Christian faith (p. 32). Of several Greek words for "love" this was uniquely used by Christians. *Agape* contrasts with *eros,* Plato's word for "love." Unlike the popular impression, it had nothing to do with "erotic" or sensual love (p. 130). A religious concept, it is *egocentric* love. "Everything centres round the individual soul and its fate" (p. 137). The dominant idea is happiness. Then Aristotle, the Hedonists, and the Stoics pursued, with some modifications, the same idea of love as having to do with such individual happiness.

Agape is the opposite of egocentrism, of such individualism. ". . . Christianity makes a revolutionary change. The question of the Good is no longer envisaged from the point of view of the isolated individual, but is widened out to cover the relations of man with God and with his fellow-men" (p. 30). *Agape* is a way of fellowship with God and with other human beings (pp. 46, 52, 104). The love of neighbor is not separate from the love of God but is to be seen as "God loving through us."

Paul Tillich takes a philosophical, ontological approach to love in his lectures, *Love, Power, and Justice.*[4] "Reuniting love" is seen as the highest form of power and of justice.

The most comprehensive study on Christian "love" since Nygren is by Gene Outka in *Agape, An Ethical Analysis.*[5] In a normative approach, he describes the thinking of many others, yet draws his own significant conclusions. He, too, is impressed with the centrality of *agape* in Christianity. He sees its influence on the life of the world as substantial, with practicable and significant meaning for contemporary problems.

What Love Is Not—And Is

On the basis of our brief look at what Scripture and scholars have to say about Christian "love," we make some observations as to what *agape* is not—and is. This should help to clear away some popular misunderstandings. As we are using the term, "love" is

NOT self-centeredness	IS self-giving for others
NOT simply individual interest	IS concern for relationships
NOT superficial sentimentality	IS deep conviction
NOT maudlin feelings	IS real empathy
NOT liking everybody	IS respecting every person
NOT "bleeding heart" posing	IS genuine compassion
NOT an emotional bath	IS firmness of commitment
NOT softheadedness	IS tough-mindedness
NOT weakness	IS strength.

In terms of ethics, Christian "love," *agape,* means: *On the basis of God's love revealed in Jesus Christ, thinking, feeling, and acting in self-giving, outgoing, spontaneous, creative, constructive, intelligent goodwill.*

Meanings of "Love" for "Peace"

From the beginning of the Good News of God in Jesus Christ, there are important connections between "love" and "peace."

Jesus came into the world not as a conquering king, but as a winsome baby, radiating and evoking "love." In the Bible story God's messengers proclaim: ". . . behold, I bring you good tidings of great joy, which shall be to all people. . . . Glory to God in the highest, and on earth, peace, good will toward men" (Luke 2:10-14, KJV). Ringing through the centuries, countless carols and Christmas messages reecho that announcement connecting the revelation of God's love to God's will for peace on earth. Think how many carols combine those ideas of "love" and "peace."

But, really, what do all the charming carols about a baby in a manger, love, goodwill, and peace have to do with the hard facts and dynamic forces of world politics, economics, human pride, greed, hatred, ambition, ethnocentrism, nationalism, and war? That precisely is one way of posing the question: Is Christian faith relevant to life—not just in the hereafter—but also in the here and now? The answer is spelled out in how we do—or do not—translate our "faith working through love" into realities in the life of human beings and of the world.

The meanings of "love" for "peace" in international life are obviously myriad. As to how "love" relates to "peace" there is a wide range of views. We cite seven: (1) "Love" is simply not practical in international affairs; so ignore it and get on with expedient, pragmatic politics. (2) The eschatological framework of the New Testament means it had an "interim ethic" for believers awaiting the imminent end of the world, but it can give no guidance for our continuing, complex time. (3) "It is impossible to construct a social ethic out of the ideal of love in its pure form, because the ideal presupposes the resolution of the conflict of life with life;"[6] so the way of love is not "realistic." (4) "Love" cannot be applied directly in international relations, but it can be applied through "middle axioms." This is like a car's transmission applying power not in direct drive but adjusting to suit different conditions. (5) In "situation ethics" one can sometimes apply "love" in particular circumstances, but not always. (6) "Love" can be an approach to international relations to be pursued at all times. (7) We are not to be guided simply by possible consequences of our actions but to live by "love" because as Christians we have no other option.

Clearly, we can here comment only briefly on those views. On the basis of our scriptural survey, the first three are unacceptable. Concerning number 3, "love" does *not* "presuppose the resolution of the conflicts of life with life" but proposes a way of working toward resolution. Choices among the other views can be congruent with our study. Readers are challenged on the basis of their own faith, views of Scripture, and analysis to clarify their own positions on the relations of "love" to international affairs. It may be one or more of the above, or something quite different. Certain functions of "love" in relation to our quest for peace, as the author sees them, are suggested below.

"Love" as a Bond in Our Work for Peace

"Love" unites us as Christians in vital relationship to God, to Jesus Christ, and to each other. Thus, we can work together for peace, in "faith, hope, and love," despite varying approaches to the meaning of "love": for ethics, positions of pacifism or not, and differences in denomination, culture, political or economic system, race, sex, or nationality. Many of us have experienced this cooperation, despite differences, as peacemakers, with Christians having widely varying views and backgrounds at local, state, national, and world levels.

Most of the crucial issues in world affairs do not involve the question of pacifism, but by their life-or-death urgency demand the best efforts of us all. In certain issues and organizations, pacifists work together with particular effectiveness.[7] The achievements of "the historic peace churches" and of "pacifist fellowships" have been of incalculable value, far out of proportion to their limited numbers. They deserve more understanding and appreciation.

However, what we are considering here is more inclusive cooperation among all Christians who share the conviction that "love" is at the heart of our faith, so that there is no elective but a divine directive that we "seek peace and pursue it." In *agape* we can find a remarkable meeting of minds on international issues, and—even when holding differing views—unique bonding, mutual reinforcing, and personal and group empowering.

"Love" as an Approach in Our Work for Peace

From our brief consideration of "love" and "peace" we see in Jesus' teaching, and elsewhere in the Bible, specific counsels for "love in action," and we see "love" as "reconciliation," as an attitude and a way of working at problems that divide people and nations. As we take up the most crucial world issues and consider what we can do, we shall see the relevance of "love" in its ideas for action and in its orientation of "reconciliation." The latter has valuable potentials for contemporary techniques, such as "conflict control," "conflict management," "conflict resolution."

It is to be hoped that we shall find "love" and "peace" increasingly combined in our lives, in our study and action, and in our world, as in the benediction: ". . .be of good comfort, be of one mind, live in peace; and the God of love and peace shall be with you" (2 Corinthians 13:11, KJV).

5

World Ministries (Missions), Service, Edu-Action— for Peace

. . . that thy way may be known upon earth,
thy saving health among all nations.
(Psalm 67:2, KJV)

When a U.S. plane was shot down on a bombing mission to Japan in World War II, one of the crew was saved from the sea by the Japanese and interned with other prisoners. They suffered malnutrition and abuse. But one Japanese captor secretly gave them food and was friendly when alone with them. The airman asked him why he was showing enemies such kindness at risk to himself. He replied, "Because I am a Christian." This made a strong impression on the young American. After the war, returning to the States, he picked up the pieces of his life and was rapidly moving up a ladder of corporate success. One day he conferred with his pastor in his home church, in Hartford, Connecticut, saying that he knew there was an important role for Christian laymen in business, but he wished to find some other form of service for his life. After more sessions, exploring many options, he came to the conviction that God's purpose was for him to be a missionary. So he went to Andover Newton Seminary. After graduation, he and his wife were commissioned as missionaries by the American Baptist Foreign Mission Society—to Japan! The mission this time; not to bring death and destruction, but life and peace. Led by the Spirit of the God of love, grateful for the sparing of his life, and remembering the quietly courageous 83

Christian who had befriended him and other war prisoners,
Stan and Evie Manierre went to Japan. Through years of ar-
duous work they rendered outstanding service. Stan won such
respect that Japanese leaders chose him to serve for a time as
executive of their National Christian Council. Their many
ministries lived out the Scripture: "How beautiful are the feet
of them that preach the gospel of peace, and bring glad tidings
of good things!" (Romans 10:15, KJV; Isaiah 52:7; Nahum 1:15).

The Great Commission

The concept of a mission to others for God goes back to the
Old Testament, as seen in Psalms, Jonah, and certain prophets
such as Isaiah. In the New Testament, Jesus, the risen Lord,
gives "the Great Commission": "Go ye into all the world, and
preach the gospel to every creature" (Mark 16:15, KJV; cf.
Matthew 28; Luke 24). "The Gospel" in New Testament Greek
equals "The Good News," which we shall use. Jesus emphasizes
practicing as well as *preaching* it (John 14–17). He says of the
believer: ". . . the works that I do shall he do also; and greater
works than these shall he do . . ." (John 14:12, KJV). At the
Last Supper he gives his disciples a longer commission: to
believe him, to love him, to keep his commandments, to win
others to believe through their words, their acts, and their
being united in love (John 17, esp. vv. 21-23).

"Doing the Gospel" is seen in the deeds and title of "The Acts
of the Apostles," or better, "The Acts of God Through the Apostles." Its action-packed dramas portray the beginnings of the
Christian world mission. God's "preaching peace by Jesus
Christ" and Jesus' "doing the Gospel" are seen in Acts 10:34-
48. Acts portrays the risen Lord projecting the ever-widening
circles of the preaching and practicing of the Good News:

> . . . ye shall receive power, after that the Holy Spirit is come upon
> you: and ye shall be witnesses unto me both in Jerusalem and in
> all Judaea, and in Samaria, and unto the uttermost part of the
> earth (Acts 1:8, KJV).

In our time, we can transcribe that in such ways as this:

> . . . and ye shall be witnesses unto me in _____(your
> town), and in _____(your state), and in the U.S.A., and
> unto the uttermost part of the earth.

Thus, the call to mission comes to each of us in our own time
and place, moving in ever larger circles around the globe.

The Glorious History of the Christian World Mission

Historical study repels many people because so much of it has been portrayed as recurring wars and truces. Fortunately, many writers and textbooks have moved from that deadly formula to the development of ideas and the way people lived. We can find truly exciting history in the unfolding story of the Christian world mission. It has been interpreted by many scholars, as seen in the vast collection of the Day Mission Library at Yale Divinity School. Especially valuable are the voluminous writings of Kenneth Scott Latourette, whose dedicated research and illuminating interpretations are symbolized in his masterwork, *A History of the Expansion of Christianity*.[1] That story begins with Christians in Judea, then widens as they carried the Good News to Constantinople, Eastern Europe, Rome, Western Europe, and other areas around the globe. It continues through "the modern missionary movement" until today there is a Christian witness in every land on Earth. For the scope, sweep, and details of that glorious story, the reader is referred to books similar to those mentioned above.

In this century the concept has become clearer, as it was in early Christianity and to some wise leaders, that Christianity is itself a mission. There is a changing use of language: The word "missions" used in "the modern missionary movement" is being replaced in referring to present operations by such terms as "overseas ministries," "international ministries," or "world ministries." With these developments the word "mission" is now increasingly used to refer to the whole work of the whole church in the whole world.

These are not just semantic changes. The terminology has tremendous implications for concepts and methods. No longer is there so much thought of "senders" and "receivers" of missions, nor of "older" and "younger" churches. Now, Christianity is increasingly seen as an interdependent worldwide community, with the bases for mission being everywhere, and with all Christians having global responsibilities. Thus, Christians in Asia, Africa, and Latin America are sending "missionaries" to various fields, including the U.S.A. and Europe. Increasingly, such contemporary emissaries are being called not "missionaries" but "fraternal workers." (That is not to say that we in the U.S.A. do not need "missionaries" to help in the preaching and practicing of Christianity!) Other implications of the changes in language are that planning is increasingly being done cooperatively; finances are being pooled; and there is more joint action in mission.

What used to be called "missions," and is now called "world ministries," is increasingly understood not to be a separate enterprise nor an elective for a few, but integral and mandatory as part of "the mission" for all Christians. "The Great Commission" is increasingly being seen as central in Christianity along with "The Great Commandment." "The mission" includes not just conversions of individuals, crucial as those are for the present and eternal life of each person and for the growth of the church, but also includes seeking, with the Good News of God, to make maximum impact on all that affects the lives of all people on Earth, including "the things that make for peace."

Since this chapter deals with the missionary enterprise in some historical perspective, largely "the modern missionary movement," we use the term "missions" as characteristic of that period, but to signify the current changes of usage, we put the term "missions" in quotation marks. We also seek where the emphasis is contemporary to use a term such as "world ministries."

Contributions of "Missions" to Peace

What has "the modern missionary movement" contributed, besides blessings in individual lives, to "the conditions of peace"?

Central to all that "missions" have done and that "world ministries" are doing is the purpose to share the Good News, faith in a universal God of love who purposes peace, justice, freedom, and a better life for all people. This means living in love toward God and toward others, as in the Great Commandment. The way of love applies not only to personal relations but also to all structures and processes of society.

As a result of "missions," "love" has been put into practice in the Christian community. The church is a living demonstration that peoples of different tribes, languages, cultures, and nations can live and work together in peace. Most dramatic are the achievements of "missions" in being instrumental in some areas in ending cannibalism, head-hunting, and slavery, and contributing uniquely in various ways to ending colonialism. It has helped, and continues to help, in the breaking down of caste systems, segregation, and discrimination; it has freed multitudes of "untouchables" from a miserable, oppressed existence to a more liberated, satisfying life. It has brought, and continues to bring, understanding among different peoples around the globe.

At the world level, also, "missions" laid much groundwork for the ecumenical movement. The world conferences of the International Missionary Council at Edinburgh in 1910 and the World Conference on Faith and Order at Lausanne in 1927 were among instrumental forces leading to the founding of the World Council of Churches in 1947. Also, from the Student Volunteer Movement and the World Student Christian Federation came a generation of leaders in the ecumenical movement. The subsequent influence of the World Council of Churches, national councils, and other ecumenical organizations for international peace is significant beyond calculation.

The missionary movement was and is an international trailblazer. It *pioneered* in such fields as the following:

INTERNATIONAL EXCHANGE OF PERSONS, for example, students, teachers.

PEACE-CORPS-TYPE WORK, with overseas youth service projects and short-term missionary programs.

TECHNICAL ASSISTANCE (long decades before governments) in:

AGRICULTURE, including increased food production;

EDUCATION;

FAMILY PLANNING, related to responsible parenthood and world population problems;

INDUSTRIAL DEVELOPMENT, initiating and humanizing it;

LANGUAGE DEVELOPMENT, related to Bible translation in more than a thousand tongues;

LITERACY, around the world;

MEDICAL SERVICES, for example, individual health care, hygiene, clinics, hospitals, and training of doctors, nurses, midwives, and health-service assistants;

NUTRITION;

PUBLIC HEALTH, including sanitation and pure water.

Now many such services are being multiplied as governments are providing "technical assistance" and "mutual aid" both internally and through international cooperation in regional organizations and in the UN system, for examples, UNDP (UN Development Programme), FAO (Food and Agriculture Organization), ILO (International Labor Organization), and WHO (World Health Organization).

Adequate recognition has yet to be given to the Christian movement for its unique roles in helping to bring an end to colonialism and the beginning of independent life to more than one hundred new nations in the mid-twentieth century. Missionaries were preaching and doing the Good News of a God who wills justice and freedom, as well as love. In the colonial areas around the globe these ideas permeated the "mission" churches, schools, and colleges. Thus, minds were excited, imaginations stimulated, attitudes enlivened, and resolves developed in hosts of believers. From this came public opinion and leadership, instrumental in shaking off the shackles of colonialism and creating new nations. Also, in schools and churches in countries which held colonies, ideas and attitudes grew for justice and freedom. These ideas contributed to action in many of these nations, helping to bring a relatively peaceful transition from imperialism to independence for the new nations.

A related, highly significant contribution of "missions" to "peace" was the training of young people who became national and world leaders with the ending of colonialism, the establishing of new nations, and the development of more international order through the UN system. Many of them received their education, health care, personal development, and knowledge of agricultural, industrial, and other dimensions of society through the work of "missions." So, in the new capitols and in the UN, at its headquarters and in posts around the globe, are many leaders who, while growing up in the former colonies, received their education and training through Christian "missions." Many of them bring new wisdom and perspective to national and world issues.

Another important contribution to peace is the large number of missionaries' sons and daughters who serve in international relations in governments, the UN system, and NGOs.

A unique service rendered by missionaries and executives is in relations with governments. This is fraught with problems: separation of church and state in the U.S.A., and possible misuse of these relations by political leaders for their own purposes. However, being careful about such problems, mission personnel have been and are performing valuable services, cooperating with governments in "the things which make for peace."

Missionaries, and mission executives, based on their knowledge and perspectives, sometimes take the initiative in conferring with governments. This is done abroad and in the U.S.A., as for instance, in the Department of State, with mutual benefits. Another service is testimony before committees of Congress on issues where mission personnel have special expertise.

Governments sometimes take the initiative in requesting church leaders, including those in "world ministries," to share their expertise. The author has firsthand knowledge of numerous examples. For instance, he was invited by the president to participate at the White House in planning for the Peace Corps. Under his direction many church organizations had conducted a study on Peace Corps ideas. This study had been sparked by students on the General Committee of the Department of International Affairs of the NCC. They had responded enthusiastically to the proposal by Senator Humphrey and Representative Reuss, months before John F. Kennedy used the idea in his presidential campaign. News of the study brought requests for reports from around the world. News of the study had reached the White House, hence the invitation. The author delegated the responsibility to a church executive with years of experience working with short-term missionaries and church youth service projects overseas. So he provided unique help to the government in laying plans for the Peace Corps.

"World ministries" also contribute to peace in what they do for supporters in local churches. Through the years, missionary programs in study groups, women's societies and circles, youth and student groups, and men's fellowships have included "mission" book reviews, discussions, fairs with photos and exhibits, and missionaries as speakers. So what does all this have to do with peace? While he was a representative in Congress, the president of New York University, Dr. John Brademas, addressed church leaders in Indiana in a Nationwide Program of Education and Action for Peace. He said that in his experience among groups of people, those in the churches working for missions are the best informed and most concerned about world affairs.

A parallel phenomenon has occurred among missionaries: Many are unusually well informed on world affairs and dedicated to peace. When Albert Schweitzer was in the heart of Africa on his mission of healing, teaching, thinking, and writing *A Philosophy of Civilization,* with World War I raging in Europe, he wrote: "I felt it every day to be a great mercy that while others had to be killing, I could not only save life but even work as well to bring nearer the coming of the Era of Peace."[2] Around the world Christians doing and supporting "missions," even in war times, have worked and continue to work for peace.

Seeking Peace Through World Service

From the beginning, Christians have engaged in world service. Paul and his colleagues collected funds for those in need in Judea (Acts 11:29; Romans 15:26; 1 Corinthians 16:1-4; 2 Corinthians 8 and 9; Galatians 2:10). In our time, world needs have become so vast that to meet human suffering in face of manmade and natural disasters, churches have set up special agencies. Protestant, Orthodox, and Roman Catholic agencies cooperate in the field and in collecting funds, as in "One Great Hour of Sharing."

As with "missions," the basic motivation for "service" is the Great Commandment given by Jesus, which means loving God and others. We are able to do that because of the Good News of the God of love.

People in local congregations contribute funds, clothing, and other goods. These are channeled by denominational cooperation through CWS (Church World Service), the coordinating, operating agency in the NCC. At the global level, coordination and operations are carried out by the World Council of Churches, with the cooperation of over two hundred denominations and many national councils, through its Division of Interchurch Aid, Refugees and World Service (DICARWS), established at the close of World War II.

After World War II, through DICARWS, economic needs in churches in war-ravaged countries were significantly met by interchurch aid. Hosts of refugees received new hope and life from heroic efforts of dedicated administrators, staffs in refugee camps, and shiploads of supplies received from churches in many countries. Then came massive resettlement in various lands, as in the U.S.A., through the Displaced Persons Program. Church people signed affidavits as sponsors so that these newcomers would not become public charges. That meant finding jobs and housing, providing other services, and giving friendship to them.

To focus on the local congregation: A "mission"-minded church in Hartford, Connecticut, took this challenge seriously in its concern for people and world affairs. It sent affidavits through the American Baptist Convention and CWS to resettle displaced persons; and started with six. It resettled them, then sent for additional people, about twelve at a time. The church signed a total of fifty-five affidavits, and within about two years, when the law permitting this expired, thirty-six persons had been resettled by that one church.

Church agencies provided other postwar services which helped to heal some of the wounds of humanity. They sent medical supplies; some of these were given by pharmaceutical companies and more were purchased through offerings. Thus Christians helped to curb disease and epidemics in the wake of war. They continue to send medical supplies for people in disasters.

Chicken farmers and church leaders in Connecticut and other states flew millions of chicks to war-ravaged areas to start flocks to provide eggs and meat for hungry people.

Other Christian farmers sent shiploads of "Heifers for Relief" to rebuild herds in areas where war had wiped them out. One moving, amusing, relevant story involved a Denison University student, just returned from war. He had been shot down on a bombing mission to Gdynia, Poland, but was miraculously saved from the sea. For summer vacation, he volunteered as an attendant on a "Heifers for Relief" boat. He was thinking that he would be aiding in a program which would provide milk and, later, meat for war-deprived children and others. He hoped this mission of peace might go to Poland. But on board, John Ward, "Zeke," found himself a nursemaid not to heifers but to mules! They did go to Poland—to Gdynia! As he told the story, Zeke smiled with amusement, but satisfaction, knowing his mules were working in fields to produce food for needy people.

(A brief personal note: Yes, a few years later, the author had the privilege of introducing Stan Manierre, cited earlier, and Zeke Ward at an American Baptist Convention session. Both had been miraculously saved from the sea when shot down on bombing missions; both had gone back for missions of peace, on opposite sides of the globe. When they met, it was like two poles of an arc light bursting into brightness to illuminate the surrounding world, as they had done on their missions of mercy. Zeke later became a missionary, with his wife, serving Indians in Nevada.)

Christian farmers in the Midwest and elsewhere, in the pattern of the biblical tithe, set aside "Lord's Acres," giving production from them to be sent to people in need overseas.

CROP (Christian Rural Overseas Program) began its ministries by sending food to people hungry from war's devastation. Soon its work became worldwide. It still significantly alleviates starvation, malnutrition, and concomitant diseases afflicting millions of people. Now it focuses more on helping people to help themselves. "Hunger walks" in communities and colleges contribute toward funds for its continuing urgent work.

Service programs, in general, were expanded beyond Europe to meet growing and more fully perceived critical needs of other peoples around the globe, making it truly "world service." Needs have been massive, responses magnanimous, and results magnificent.

World service became increasingly oriented toward eliminating basic causes of human suffering. It continues to meet relief needs, but it is also helping people to help themselves, for example, by improving agriculture, water supply, and reforestation.

We would also pay tribute to major achievements of others. With longer experience in humanitarian ministries, "the historic peace churches," the Church of the Brethren, the Mennonites, and the American Friends Service Committee, continue their remarkable work around the globe. The Roman Catholic Church carries on massive world relief services. Other religious agencies, such as those of the Unitarian Universalist Association and Jewish organizations, have been active in various service projects.

Christians in other lands sponsor significant service programs, such as Oxfam from Britain and *Brot für die Welt* from Germany. (These programs are now also represented in the U.S.A.)

A number of other voluntary organizations, governments,

and the UN system have increasingly engaged in similar services.

Results of World Service for People—and for Peace

What have all these efforts added up to? More than it is possible to calculate, either in monetary or in human terms. Concentrating on the work of DICARWS and CWS and related agencies, we can sketch some achievements of the last four decades.

In local congregations, scores of millions of Christians in this and other lands have given and continue to contribute on offering plates: loose change, folding money, and large checks, adding up in value to many hundreds of millions of dollars. Christian farmers have contributed countless chicks, eggs, heifers, pigs, horses, mules, and seeds, providing chains of life beyond computation. Christians, through giving, have flown and shipped those hatching and walking food factories around the globe. They have sent mountains of medicine, bandages, clothing, shoes, blankets, tents, and other supplies for relief and rehabilitation, and continue to do so. All this adds up to more service to those in need than ever before in history.

What have been the results for human beings? Countless persons, the world around, were and are being healed with the aid of medical supplies. Tens of millions of refugees were and are being served and resettled. More millions of people were and are being saved from starvation and accompanying diseases—many from premature death. Multitudes suffering from earthquakes, floods, hurricanes, typhoons, droughts, famines, epidemics, and other disasters were and are being given new hope and life. We can imagine only a small fraction of the blessings of world service to the lives of hundreds of millions of people.

The magnanimous, continuing responses of contemporary Christians to world needs are a modern multiplication of the experiences of the early churches. Paul wrote about "the favor of God" in the "wealth of generosity" of the churches which gave "to the utmost of their ability . . . and beyond it." He said, "they did far more than I hoped." The secret? They first "gave themselves to the Lord . . ." (2 Corinthians 8:1-5, Goodspeed). In world service is demonstrated a reliving of the acts of God through the apostles in the latter half of the twentieth century.

Rejoicing in what has been done for people in their needs, still we are humbled as we recall Jesus' saying in Luke 17:10 (KJV): "So likewise ye, when ye shall have done all those things which are commanded you, say, We are unprofitable servants: we have done that which was our duty to do."

Staggering as all statistics may be of what has been done, more staggering are the continuing and, indeed, increasing human needs in almost every land, including our own. The urgency for even more generous response continues, calling to our hearts—and minds—for ever-expanding efforts to meet the multiplying needs among our fellow human beings through world service.

But what has all this to do with peace? Beyond religious duties and human concerns, these ministries in world service have contributed and will continue to contribute significantly to peace. They increase justice, freedom, and humanization in the world, all making for peace. They increase, in those who give and those who receive, the amounts of goodwill, of love on Earth. Clearly, these are essential to world community and peace.

Edu-Action

A third dimension of the work of the churches for peace is education oriented to action. For this we suggest the shorthand term, EDU-ACTION. It denotes combining theory and practice, theology and praxis, faith and life. Such ministries are led by agencies of various names in denominations and ecumenical organizations: for example, "Christian Social Concerns," "Christian Life and Work," "Church and Society," "Peace Concerns Program," and "Christian Social Education and Action." Significantly, *both* education and action are emphasized through such agencies.

"Christian education" is found in most churches. Often, however, much time has been put into studying biblical and theological matters (which are essential) and little into practical issues and plans for action (which are also essential). We stress the growing need for Christian education *and* the increasing urgency for it to be more action-oriented.

Action as an antidote for fear is stressed by psychologists. The author, in an address to a conference at the U.S. Department of State, proposed *informed action* as a way to deal with what seems to be public apathy. Actually, beneath this seeming apathy are fear of nuclear war, frustration in not knowing what to do, and futility in despairing that anything can be done. As people are shown that informed action can be effective in world affairs, they can work their way out of apathy into responsible learning and action.

Note *"informed action."* Some actions can be simply frenetic and ineffective. It is imperative that we know *why* we are acting, based on our faith from the Bible and theological reflection. This will sustain us when the going is long and hard, as might cause fainter hearts and heads to fall by the wayside, and will enable us to persevere in "pursuing peace." (Many "peace movements" have burgeoned, then withered because they lacked sufficient theological or philosophical roots.) It is likewise essential that we know *what* the issues are. Further, it is indispensable that we know *how* we can act on them effectively. Hence we see the wisdom, indeed the utter necessity, for the church to emphasize "Christian social *education and action.*"

The divine imperative for thought and action is seen in the Great Commandment. We recall that Jesus said, about thinking, "'You shall love the Lord your God . . . with all your mind'"; and, about acting, "'You shall love your neighbor,'" for which he spelled out specifics (Matthew 22:37-39; chaps. 5–7). Paul later stressed "faith acting through love" (Galatians 5:6, Goodspeed). It is "true love, which shows itself in action" (1 John 3:18, *Good News Bible*). Or, for directness, consider "The Cotton Patch Version":[3] ". . . let's not *talk* about love. Let's not *sing* about love. Let's put love into *action* and make it *real.*"

The combined emphasis on thought and action is seen as religious imperative in the thinking of Dag Hammarskjöld. He had profound regard for Christian mystics, such as Thomas à Kempis and his meditations *The Imitation of Christ.* But he stressed the need for faith to go into action, in *Markings:* "In our era, the road to holiness necessarily passes through the world of action."[4] On the kind of action needed, the philosopher John Macmurray said, in essence, "All knowledge is for the sake of action; and all action is for the sake of people."[5]

At the global level, education and action for peace have been led by the World Council of Churches through its units, such as DICARWS, Church and Society, Justice and Service, and especially the CCIA (Commission of the Churches on International Affairs). The pioneering statesmanship of the CCIA's early leaders, including its Director O. Frederick Nolde, Executive Secretary Richard M. Fagley, and its Chairman Sir Kenneth Grubb, set an excellent standard for its work which has continued with effectiveness.

Also, religious world bodies deal with some peace responsibilities at the global level. These include, for example, the Anglican Consultation Council and the Lambeth Conference of Bishops of the Anglican Communion, the Baptist World Alliance, the heads of the Eastern Orthodox Churches, the Friends World Committee for Consultation, the Lutheran World Federation, the Mennonite World Conference, the World Alliance of Reformed Churches (Presbyterian and Congregational), the World Convention of Churches of Christ, the World Methodist Council, the World Council of Synagogues (Conservative) and the World Union of Progressive Judaism.

At the national level, in the U.S.A., the NCC and its constituent communions lead in education and action programs for peace. The NCC works through its units such as the Division of Overseas Ministries, CWS, the Commission on Justice, Liberation, and Human Fulfillment, and the Division of Church and Society, particularly its Office on International Affairs. Many denominations have units which develop, coordinate, and promote work for peace, including channeling programs from the NCC to their local churches. In annual programming for peace, the NCC and these church bodies usually focus primarily on three or four major issues, to make for more concentrated study and more effective action.

Intermediate mechanisms are conciliar and denominational: state and local councils of churches, or interfaith conferences, usually have committees related to peace. Denominations have conventions, associations, dioceses, classes, districts, synods, presbyteries or other structures, often with units on peace.

The ultimate focus is the local church and its members. Program materials are planned for them appropriate to the current emphases. Continuous communication with local churches includes notes in ecumenical and denominational periodicals, newsletters, and special bulletins about government decisions pending on relevant issues. Several qroups coordinate efforts through IMPACT, a publication which alerts readers to what decisions are being made in the U.S. Government on such issues. In this way, public opinion can be focused at points and times at which it will be the most influential.

Congregations have a wide variety of organizational patterns depending on denominational, local, and other factors. In American Baptist Churches, responsibilities for peace programming may be in a Church Council, the Board of Christian Education, the Board of Deacons, a Committee on Christian Social Concerns, a Missionary Education Committee, or a task force on peace. In most American Baptist churches, the responsible group, or the pastor, or both cooperatively, channel the program materials from the WCC and NCC and various denominational units, such as the ABC Peace Concerns Program, into the local congregation. In the United Methodist Church, congregations have a chairperson of Church and Society who is a member of the Council on Ministries and has opportunities to develop task forces on peace and other Christian social concerns. They receive materials and guidance from the highly effective General Board of Church and Society. Some other denominations have similar patterns of structure and programming.

A parallel structure from national to local levels is found in women's societies in many denominations. Worthy of special note are the powerful organization of United Methodist Women and the Women's Division of the General Board of Global Ministries in the United Methodist Church. The United Methodist Women work at national, district, and local congregational levels in effective ways.

Church Women United, which is related to the NCC, should be recognized for outstanding work in national leadership for study and action on peace, in relation to the UN, and in the annual World Day of Prayer and World Community Day.

On the importance of the local church and its members in "edu-action" for peace, "not much really happens until it happens locally." This will be discussed more fully in chapter 8.

Getting It All Together

Have you heard of church members opening their purses for collections for "missions" in Africa but not opening their minds, hearts, churches, or equal opportunities in their communities to Americans whose ancestors were forcibly brought from Africa? Or do you know of those who give to "missions" in Africa but are not concerned for the cruel degradation of *apartheid* in South Africa and so do business with corporations which aid and comfort that regime?

Have you heard of church members giving for relief through "world service" but failing to be interested in Christian "edu-action" to reduce causes of such needs? This is like running an ambulance service for victims in cars crashing over a cliff but not putting up a guard rail to prevent accidents. We as Christians do respond to emergency calls; but it is imperative that we also do all in our power, under God, through "edu-action" for peace, to create a world which will reduce such needs.

Equally insufficient would be "edu-action" without supporting "missions" and "service" for meeting human spiritual and physical needs.

Some ask, "Why not concentrate only on 'missions' and 'service' instead of dealing with 'government,' 'politics,' and 'foreign aid'?" The answer: We must be concerned with *all* these, because *all* that can be done by *all* "missions" programs and *all* "service" of *all* churches can meet *only a fraction* of global need. Human suffering is so vast that the *combined* resources of churches *and* other NGOs *and* governments *and* the UN are required!

As to governments, Christians and churches have responsibilities for influencing them to reduce excessive spending for military aid and to provide more funds for world economic and social development, to meet human need, and to promote peace.

Churches also have unique roles in making the most efficient use of "world ministries" and "service" funds. Acting in good stewardship, churches can create imaginative "pilot projects" which prove so successful that they are taken up by governments and the UN, on a broader scale with much larger funds. This happened dramatically in work for literacy, in industrial training for youth in refugee camps, and in reforestation on the edge of the Sahara Desert. There, in a "world service" pilot project, unemployed men, in exchange for food for their families, planted trees; this made them and "the desert . . . rejoice, and blossom as the rose" (Isaiah 35:1, KJV).

It is imperative for those of us concerned for "peace" to support "world ministries," to share in "world service," and to do "edu-action." All three are synergistic components of *the*

Christian mission, of work for *all* of us to share in. All three are interrelated and indispensable to "the whole gospel for the whole person for the whole world." All three demand our prayers, followed by "putting shoes on our prayers" by giving our thinking, our talents, our time, our money, our goods—but first giving ourselves (2 Corinthians 8:5). Thus, increasingly, God's "way may be known upon earth," that is, God's "saving health among all nations" (Psalm 67:2, KJV).

From our brief survey it is clear that you who have supported "world ministries" ("missions"), you who have contributed to "world service," and you who have shared in "edu-action" have done more for "peace" than most people, and possibly you, have ever realized.

Thrice blessed are you who particpate in "world ministries" *and* "service" *and* "edu-action," for you have found practical ways to love God and your neighbors around the world, and to "seek peace and pursue it." Your prayers, thoughts, and actions are being multiplied in God's economy, will, and work for peace, justice, freedom, and humanization.

But so much more remains to be done!

"Church and State" and Foreign Policy

Render . . . unto Caesar the things which are Caesar's; and unto God the things that are God's.

(Matthew 22:21, KJV)

THE SCENE: The Cabinet Room in the White House.

THE CAST OF CHARACTERS: President Kennedy; Secretary of State, Dean Rusk; their Public Liaison Officer, Harry Seamans; and a few selected national and world church leaders.

THE OCCASION: "The Appeal to All Governments and Peoples," from the World Council of Churches' Assembly at New Delhi, being presented to the U.S. and other governments.

THE AGENDA: Some of the most crucial life-and-death problems: disarmament, including nuclear and conventional weapons; and world economic and social development.

A QUESTION over which President Kennedy was agonizing: Should the U.S.A. continue testing nuclear weapons or seek a treaty with the U.S.S.R. for cessation? The factors he was weighing were the damages to health and life and the heightening threats of war by testing versus possible risks to national security by seeking a test-ban treaty.

A CHURCH-STATE ISSUE: Three times the president spoke of his agonizing over that question. A church leader, seeking to express empathy, mis-spoke, saying, "Mr. President, whatever your decision, we will support you." With sharp insight, the president replied, "Maybe in the decision I must make you cannot support me." (Fortunately, his eventual decision for 101 bilateral cessation was one the churches had been advocating, so could support.) Continuing, the president spoke of decision makers for the state and for the church having differing responsibilities. In response, the author quoted to the president the counsel Secretary Rusk had given at a church conference: "Support us where you can; criticize us where you must." The president and the church leaders agreed with that as part of a practicable formula for relations of church to state on foreign policy. Other important relations include: demonstrating to government the need for new policies or revision of existing ones, and influencing where necessary and possible the formulation and administration of policy.

Some Biblical, Theological, and Political Questions

In relation to the state, Christians have tended to stress two differing lines of thought found in the Bible: *Opposing* the state as evil, citing Revelation 13 and Acts 5:29 (KJV), "We ought to obey God rather than men." *Obedience* to the state, citing Romans 13:1, with the premise that "the powers that be are ordained of God," and concluding, "Render therefore to all their dues" (13:7) is used to support this stance (cf. 1 Peter 2:13-17; Titus 3:1). The saying of Jesus in the epigraph is not so clear. It is variously interpreted by the two sides. But there is consensus on one meaning: ultimately all things belong not to Caesar but to God. This is supported by the passages saying that governments have powers under God.

Through the centuries, Christians, depending on their understandings of Scripture and their experiences under different governments, have developed various views on relating faith to society. In his classic, *Christ and Culture*,[1] H. Richard Niebuhr cites five of them: Christ above culture; Christ against culture; Christ identified with culture; Christ and culture in paradox; Christ transforming culture. The viewpoint in this book, and likely that of most who read it, is the last. Christians and churches have not only the right but also the responsibility to seek to improve the culture, including governments—local, state, national—and their joint efforts in the UN and other international organizations. That means seeking to influence public policies and programs so that they are as congruent as possible with the values which are basic to these Christians and churches.

In the U.S.A. the "separation of church and state" as seen in the First Amendment to the Constitution provides protection for both state and church: it provides protection for the state, that it will not be controlled by any one form of religion; and it provides protection for religious groups, that none need fear governmental domination and that all are free to practice their faith. Separation of church and state does not mean insulation of government from the influence of religion. People of various faiths serve in government, and their perspectives, attitudes, and values bear on their decision-making or other duties. Also, those in government usually welcome informed counsel from competent religious leaders. Separation of church and state does pose problems for religious groups seeking to influence the state.

The Church or the Churches?

Having used the classic phrase "church and state," we now move to more precise language. The U.S.A. is a pluralistic society, with more than 250 denominations of Christians, three major branches of Judaism, and growing numbers of people of other religions. So, there is need to be specific. In this book "the churches" will refer generally to what have been called "main line" denominations, such as the more than thirty which cooperate through the National Council of the Churches of Christ in the U.S.A., and it also includes the conciliar groups at the world, national, state, and local levels. Within the denominations we have all those levels in mind, also, but especially their local congregations and individual members. This definition is meant not to be exclusive in our approach to religion, nor to set others beyond our sense of fellowship. However, in this slim volume space dictates this specific focus.

Even within this circle, denominations and individuals have varieties of views on international topics. Some people have questioned whether the churches could hold common views on such issues. Actually, through the World and National Councils of Churches, they have achieved a remarkable consensus on most of the urgent international questions. This has been accomplished by cooperative study and action through decades. Representatives of denominations study in advance, then deliberate on such matters in the ecumenical organization through democratic processes and debate; they then adopt statements of policy commended for study and action. While respecting the rights of the minority, these decisions usually reflect views of a large majority.

Approaches to International Questions

In this chapter we look at major issues related to U.S. foreign policy on which the churches have concentrated. We have chosen that from among the options for dealing with international questions. At least two other approaches are inviting, but each would be a major undertaking beyond our purview here.

One would be to deal with "hot spots" on the globe. These heat up, sometimes blow up, sometimes continue to simmer; they keep being replaced by others in the public's attention. We make reference to this approach because it is imperative that churches and Christians be informed on such crises and seek to take the most responsible actions possible to help reduce or eliminate conflicts and to increase international cooperation. The reader is encouraged to follow publications of the WCC, the NCC, and her or his denomination to keep *au courant* with the concerns of the churches on succeeding crises around the globe.

Another approach would be to seek to deal with the *numerous* "things that make for peace." We set forth in chapter 8 a sample shopping list from which congregations and individuals may wish to choose subjects for programs or personal pursuit.

To organize our thinking and acting for peace and to seek maximum immediate relevance and effectiveness of the following, let us consider: (1) Main outlines of U.S. foreign policy; (2) How the churches have reacted to them; and (3) Related, consistent concerns of the churches, or *leitmotifs* in their work.

It should be emphasized that such an approach can cover only a portion of the responsibilities of churches and Christians as we "seek peace and pursue it." Immense dimensions beyond the specific issues of foreign policy include such concerns as constantly analyzing and working to improve the political, economic, and social orders of individual nations and of the world. We are to be concerned with systems and institutions of society, with "principalities, [and] powers" (Ephesians 6:12). Our responsibilities include working to transform these orders of the world, under God, for more order, justice, freedom, and humanization.

Here we must limit ourselves to the more immediate issues of U.S. foreign policy and what we can do about them.

Main Outlines of U.S. Foreign Policy

Foreign policy includes four levels: *Presuppositions* are the essential values, such as democracy and the primary worth of the individual person. They also include perceptions of the attitudes and resources of one's own nation and of possible allies and adversaries. *Purposes* include such goals as "peace, with justice and freedom." *Policies* set forth broad generalities of objectives for fulfilling the purposes. *Programs* are the ways policies are made real, defined by budgets and staffs.

We limit discussion here, only because of space constraints, mostly to the third level, the substance of policies. However, it should be emphasized that the churches have been, and all peacemakers should be, concerned about *all four levels* of foreign policy. Likewise with *style, posture,* and *rhetoric.*

The major profile of U.S. foreign policy at the first three levels has remained much the same in general terms from the post-World War II era. There have been many variations in style, rhetoric, and emphasis, as evidenced in programs in various administrations. These have been related to personalities, party politics, coming and going of "the cold war," changing competitions in arms, economics, and politics, and differing strategies and tactics in the East-West and in the North-South power struggles. However, most of the main outlines in policies, at the third level, with which we are primarily concerned here, have persisted since the articulation of the "containment" doctrine in 1947. This doctrine was designed for policy in Europe but was soon expanded by the "Truman Doctrine" to cover Greece and Turkey, and, indeed, much of the rest of the world. The generally persisting main outlines of U.S. foreign policy are:

1. Strengthening the UN and international institutions.

2. Supporting and strengthening Western Europe.

3. Containing expansionist efforts of Communist-dominated countries by diplomatic, political, economic, social, and ideological means, including strategic use of "foreign aid."

4. Containing expansionist efforts of Communist-dominated countries by the buildup of military might, designed in the first instance for deterrence.

5. Paradoxically seeking disarmament, negotiating on international reduction and regulation of all arms, both nuclear and conventional, while at the same time arming.

6. Helping, through trade and aid, the developing nations to help themselves in economic and social development.

The Carter administration added a new basic emphasis, which is stated as follows:

7. Human rights are to be a central consideration in U.S. foreign policy concerns and decisions.

The rationale for number seven included the centrality of human rights in U.S. history and philosophy and the possible influence of such an emphasis on other nations and the world community.

Different administrations have changed emphases and priorities. For example, the Truman, Eisenhower, and Kennedy administrations all stated that the UN was "the cornerstone of U.S. foreign policy"; under Johnson, this was eroded by concentration on the Vietnam conflict; and under Nixon and Kissinger, and since, except in the Carter administration, the UN and international institutions have been persistently neglected and even downgraded in the formulation and implementation of U.S. foreign policy.

Another obvious change is that there was a strong emphasis on foreign aid for peaceful, constructive purposes in the administrations of Truman (including his "Point Four Program" for sharing U.S. "know-how" in technical assistance projects), Eisenhower, and Kennedy. In succeeding administrations, again except for that of Carter, there has been reduced emphasis on concern and aid for the developing areas of the world.

In relations with the Communist-dominated countries, from the Kennedy through the Carter administrations there was an emphasis on detente, led by the U.S.A., between the Western bloc and the Soviet bloc; of importance also in this policy has been a renewal of relations with China.

In relation to the seven major points of U.S. foreign policy, the churches have been in general agreement, except for divided views among them on number 4 regarding military aspects of containment. The historic peace churches persistently have opposed number 4, the emphasis on military might; and other churches at times have done so especially in relation to the Vietnam conflict, the arms race, and the stress on military and defense-support foreign aid, in contrast to and often at the sacrifice of economic and social aid.

The churches have placed their strongest emphasis on the following: number 1, the UN and international institutions; number 5, disarmament; number 6, development; and number 7, human rights. In the late 1940s the churches generally supported number 2, strengthening of Western Europe, especially by the Marshall Plan and, to a lesser degree, by NATO. There has not been as much debate in latter years about support for Western Europe, although more voices have been raised recently advocating reduction of U.S. forces in Europe and opposing U.S. emplacement of new nuclear weapons there.

Concerning number 3 on relations with Communist-dominated countries, the churches have advocated that policies, and posture, style, and rhetoric as well, move from the competitive mode toward cooperation wherever possible. Competition should stress peaceful dimensions, not military brinksmanship nor arms races. Cooperation carries with it the ideas of reducing tensions, of building more constructive relationships, and of seeking to influence the Communist-dominated countries toward change which would be significant for human values within their nations and for more concord in international relations.

We now highlight five basic issues which the churches have emphasized over the years in relation to U.S. foreign policy. Four of them have already been referred to above in relation to the main outlines of U.S. foreign policy: disarmament, development, human rights, and international organization. The other emphasis comprises several components: relief, rehabilitation, refugees, and immigration.

In such a brief work we must deal with the views and actions of the churches regarding these subjects in general terms. For specifics on myriad church position statements and on evolving issues of concern being dealt with in congress and in changing administrations, the reader is referred to the WCC, the NCC, and her or his denomination. Other key NGOs also give current information. (See Resources.)

Disarmament

Disarmament is one of the most crucial life-or-death issues confronting the U.S.A. and the human race. Its urgency, starkly emphasized by nuclear weapons, is clear from reports of scientists as to the possible results of nuclear war: It would destroy most of the human beings and civilizations of the northern hemisphere and have devastating effects on the peoples of the southern hemisphere, do violence to the biosphere, and possibly mean the total extinction of the human race and most other life on Earth.[2] But continuing concern needs to include *all* arms: (1) the ABC weapons, primarily atomic (nuclear), but also the biological and chemical means of mass murder—these all contribute to the world's deadly fascination with war and the various potentials for human destruction; and (2) the whole range of conventional armaments and military forces—even without nuclear weapons, they could devastate much of the world.

A definition of what we mean by "disarmament" is important. Some people do not even wish to use the term because they think of it as one nation unilaterally disposing of its arms, which they hold would make it vulnerable to blackmail or attack and conquest. Others confuse disarmament with nations at the close of World War I and World War II simply discarding mountains of weapons they felt had become irrelevant. Our definition of disarmament does not include either of those ideas. We use it as shorthand for: *A process of international reduction and regulation of all armaments, by agreement among all concerned parties, down to levels for internal security, but insufficient for war against other nations.*

A relevant concept of Dean Rusk, former secretary of state, is "turning down the arms race" to move toward disarmament. Increasing numbers of people believe that the first step is a "nuclear freeze": an agreement by the U.S.A. and the U.S.S.R. to halt development and production of nuclear weapons with verification and not go above present levels. Other nuclear nations and potential ones should be included in this agreement. A "nuclear freeze" could prevent further stockpiling of the many times "overkill" already possessed by both "superpowers"; it could also slow the development of new and more terrifying weapons systems which threaten to make the arms race veritably uncontrollable.

Since the Hague Peace Conferences at the turn of the century, disarmament has been talked about endlessly, negotiated occasionally, but honored more in words than in deeds. A major focus in the 1950s and 1960s included the rival proposals of the U.S.A. and the U.S.S.R. for "General and Complete Disarmament." While there has been little action on that broad subject, there have been some agreements limiting arms; on the peaceful uses of space; on Antarctica as a nuclear-free zone; on the cessation of nuclear testing in the atmosphere, space, and seas; and on measures in the Strategic Arms Limitation Talks (SALT I and II). The latter measures were observed by both the U.S.S.R. and the U.S.A., even with the U.S.A. defaulting on ratification.

Strategic Arms Reduction Talks (START) began in 1982 between the U.S.A. and the U.S.S.R.

The UN completed a General Assembly Special Session on Disarmament, also in 1982, as another of its many continuing disarmament efforts. This meeting reflected the increasing concern of the major powers and of the developing nations. There is growing realization that a nuclear war would mean worldwide devastation and possibly extinction of human life. There is increasing recognition that the arms race continues to heighten international tensions. Also, there is rising concern that additional nations have produced nuclear weapons, and that about twenty more can do so. All this multiplies the possibilities of wars being unleashed by human emotional failures, terrorism, technical mishaps, or other kinds of accidents.

Alarm grows, too, at the proportion of the wealth of nations and of the world's resources being squandered on arms. The annual expenditures by the developed nations for military purposes, over $541 billion, contrast with those for foreign economic aid, approximately $35.9 billion.[3] Conclusion? Military spending is a major hindrance to world economic and social development. If such arms expenditures could be reduced, even by a small percentage at the start of the process of arms reduction, with some of the savings applied to development, a tremendous difference could be made in the deprived conditions under which two-thirds of the human race exist. The striking success which the Marshall Plan was for Europe could then be parallel in other areas on a worldwide scope; thus a marvelous new era of economic and social development would begin around the whole globe! Even the richest nations would reap vast benefits and be able to reduce economic and other problems.

Both the developed and the developing nations have responsibilities for reducing arms. Many billions of dollars worth of weapons are sold each year by the U.S.A. and the U.S.S.R., as the major merchants of death, and by other arms-producing powers. This drains resources from the poorer areas which cannot afford this military madness at the expense of their economic and social development. In this arms traffic, the bigger powers engage in high-pressure salesmanship, and the rulers of many smaller nations waste major amounts of their scarce resources on jet fighters and bombers, warships and military hardware even as the multitudes of their people are starving, malnourished, sick, and in desperate need. So, *both* major powers *and* developing nations have responsibilities to move away from such irrationality, to reduce the flow and buildup of arms among *all* nations, large and small.

But what grounds are there for any hope of ever achieving significant measures of disarmament, given the world's political antagonisms? Why should the U.S.S.R. or the U.S.A. or other nations want to reduce arms? The answer is not in idealism but realism: The leaders of the U.S.S.R. and their satellites know that disarmament would be in the self-interest of their nations. First, it would reduce the danger of their being utterly destroyed. It would reduce international tensions. It would give them and their peoples more sense of security by reducing threats of war. It would enable them, by cutting down on the vast costs for arms and the economic waste involved in a warfare state, to improve the economic lot of their peoples. (The Communist-dominated areas have perennial problems in not being able to supply enough food, housing, and consumer needs for their peoples.) The same advantages serve the self-interest of the U.S.A. and our allies—and of other nations as well. So there are practical grounds for hopes for disarmament because it is in the self-interest of all nations. A rational, reliable system of disarmament could mean eliminating the constant threat and fear of mass death of most, and possibly all, of the world's people; reducing world tensions and improving international relations; cutting the disastrous amounts of over half a trillion dollars being poured out annually in wasteful, nonproductive military expenditures; and, by moving from a warfare to a human welfare economy, helping to meet the desperate needs of literally billions of people. This last could be done by devoting vastly increased billions of dollars to agricultural improvement, education, health, housing, industrial development, medical services, social progress, and all aspects of humanization for a more abundant life for most of the human family.

Some interpret arms to be the *result* of war-breeding factors. Others consider arms as a *cause* of war-breeding factors—and of war. The latter cite the history of "arms races" which have exploded into wars. The author prefers a both-and approach, seeing truth in both of these ideas. Thus, we work for disarmament to help eliminate one of the primary causes of war and one of the major threats to survival and the quality of life. Also, we work seriously on the economic, ideological, political, psychological, and social realities which lead nations to pile up such monstrous forces of death against other peoples. Thus our concerns for disarmament lead to the whole range of basic international issues.

In light of all this, it is most appropriate that the churches have worked at disarmament as a priority issue. Based on biblical imperatives from a God of order, life, and peace, and on current Christian concerns for survival and the quality of life, the churches have consistently called and worked for disarmament. They have been at the forefront of all organizations as they have been laboring, in season and out of season, through many decades, for a dependable system of disarmament. They have been seeking international reduction and regulation of all armaments to the minimal feasible levels, concurrently with the development of world structures to provide security for all peoples.

The enormity of the problem and the urgency with which we need to do something about public policy is illustrated by an example from the United States: The Reagan administration embarked on the largest peacetime military buildup in U.S. history, totaling more than $1,500,000,000,000 (ONE AND ONE-HALF *TRILLION* DOLLARS) over five years.[4] Economically, this posed disaster in increasing inflation, providing fewer jobs per capita for expenditures, and forcing vaster cutbacks in social services for the people. To help finance this tremendous buildup, the administration planned to take away more than $300,000,000 (three hundred million dollars) from domestic programs for human needs.

Clearly, it is increasingly imperative that churches and other organizations, Christians and other people, in the U.S.A. and in other lands, use every possible influence on the governments of the U.S.A., the U.S.S.R., and all other nations around the world to take effective steps for reduction and regulation of all arms, leading toward disarmament.

Development

Another of the most crucial life-or-death issues, interrelated with disarmament as we have seen, is world economic and social development. This literally means life or death for hundreds of millions of people in the developing areas, faced with starvation, malnutrition, related diseases—and early death. But it can also profoundly affect people in the developed areas, in the quality of their life and in the possibility of death or disability if wars break out from frustrations in other areas.

An example of one type of danger was the tragedy of the Malvinas or the Falkland Islands. The Argentine junta sought, in the age-long device, to divert the people's attention from their economic woes by a "patriotic" military move. It cost many deaths, disabilities, and heartbreaks for both the Argentines and the British. It was a vast economic loss for both nations. It had ill effects on the quality of life of people in both countries, and in others in our interdependent world.

Development, since the middle of this century, has been, like disarmament, talked about endlessly, acted upon occasionally, but honored more in words than in deeds. A major focus on it, too, came through the 1950s and 1960s. Under President Truman in 1949, the U.S.A. led in sharing "know-how" with the developing areas, as we noted previously. This concept of "technical assistance" electrified the world so it was taken up by the UN and its specialized agencies. Then President Eisenhower brought about major initiatives in "foreign aid" or "mutual aid," which he preferred to call it, as he told the author and two other church leaders in a personal conference on the subject at the White House. Grants and loans for "mutual assistance" followed "technical assistance" because it was realized, for example, that if a man were taught to plow, it would be important for him to have a plow. In an address to the UN in 1953, Eisenhower also proposed the concept of "atoms-for-peace," part of which was to be of benefit to the developing nations. Also at the UN, in 1961, President Kennedy proposed a "Decade of Development," which was received enthusiastically. While less successful than hoped for, due considerably to the later diversion of U.S. thought and resources to the Vietnam conflict, the concept was renewed by the UN for the 1970s, then for a third decade for the 1980s. Over the past thirty-five years, achievements have been substantial, but they are still only a fraction of all that needs to be done.

Of special concern to the developing nations have been such other programs as UNCTAD (the UN Conference on Trade and Development) and the UN sessions related to "a new economic order." From the "Law of the Sea" negotiations, developing nations had hoped that returns from the oceans' rich resources would help to provide more adequate funding for the UN and for their economic progress. But the U.S.A. under the new administration in 1981 reduced such hopes when it retreated from the commitments to which the U.S.A. had agreed.

Under that administration there was also decreased emphasis on U.S. use of government funds for cooperation in economic and social development. At the Cancun Conference on World Development and elsewhere, President Reagan emphasized the kind of self-centered thinking which Adam Smith expounded in the eighteenth century, as he talked about "the magic of the market" for development. This thinking fails to recognize the fact that practically no private funds have gone into economic infrastructures of needy areas since the early part of this century! The source for financing such basic elements as harbors, docks, roads, bridges, education, training, health services, and transportation has been and can only continue to be primarily from governments, internally, and in "mutual aid." Obviously, private enterprise has had and will continue to have indispensable, major roles in stages above the infrastructure. "Trade," part of the lifeblood of economies, is more substantial than "aid." But *both* are needed. Private capital investments as well as "mutual aid" grants and loans are indispensable for advanced development. Both public and private participation, integrated in strategic planning, are essential for world economic and social development.

The U.S.A. has been generous in total amounts contributed in "mutual aid" programs, considerably more generous than any other nation in history. But, as the richest nation in the world, it is not carrying its weight; instead of ranking in the first place among donor countries in percent of GNP contributed for development it ranks twelfth![5]

The world has suffered repeated discouragements at the faltering of U.S.A. initiative with regard to development, at times over past years, but it still has some basic hope. A fundamental question is: Will the U.S.A. renew its commitment to world economic and social development and again give leadership-in-partnership—moral, spiritual, and financial—as it has done on previous occasions, to create more of "the conditions of peace"?

The churches around the world in general and in the United States in particular, with leadership from the WCC NCC, have kept "development" as a priority on their agenda for pursuing peace. They have done so on the basis of biblical demands from a God of justice and of caring for the disadvantaged. They have been at the forefront among all organizations, in season and out of season, in seeking more rational and larger programs for world economic and social development. They have pressed for global and national strategies involving both trade and aid policies, emphasizing the reduction of military and "defense support" foreign aid and the increase of economic and social "mutual aid" programs, to be planned and carried out to the maximum extent possible through multilateral rather than bilateral channels. They have zeroed in on combating human hunger as a specific target, with increasing emphasis on total economic and social development and making the world's economic orders more equitable.

The population explosion continues, especially in the less developed areas; there are more hungry, needy, and ill people than ever on our planet; and the rich nations are getting richer, the poor nations poorer, in relative terms. So it is more imperative than ever that churches and other organizations, and Christians and other people, in the U.S.A. and in other lands, use every possible influence at our command to provide more economic and social development to "love our neighbors" around the globe.

Human Rights

One of the major twentieth-century trends, beginning with the UN Charter in 1945, is the concern for human rights. (See the section on "Humanization" in chapter 3 for more details.)

Here we treat the issue with regard to U.S. foreign policy and related work of the churches.

At the San Francisco Conference for drafting the UN Charter, the U.S.A. and some Latin American countries took a strong stand, along with crucial urging by religious groups, so concerns for human rights were written into the Charter.

In the International Declaration of Human Rights, adopted by the UN, December 10, 1947, the U.S.A. played a leading role, again with staunch support from religious groups.

In the drafting of the International Covenants on Civil and Political Rights and on Economic, Social and Cultural Rights (1953), the U.S.A. abdicated its world leadership in human rights because of internal politics and racism.

In the Kennedy Administration the U.S.A. resumed some measured cooperation on such matters at the UN; but it specified it did not intend to join the covenants on human rights.

In the Johnson administration crucial decisions on human rights, such as the Civil Rights Act of 1964 and the Voting Rights Act of 1965, were made, but foreign policy was largely consumed with the Vietnam conflict.

In the Nixon administration, the U.S.A. faltered again in its global leadership and failed to participate in a number of significant world initiatives through the UN.

The Carter Administration's reassertion of strong U.S.A. world leadership for human rights in both policy and practice became a major dynamic force at the UN and around the world. References to human values, human rights, and human development multiplied in meetings, books, and the media. An example was a typical city newspaper's well-documented lead editorial: "Humanizing the World."[6]

President Carter's world leadership for human rights was in the highest tradition of our nation. The Declaration of Independence, with world perspective, stated that its authors owed "a decent respect to the opinions of mankind." George Washington in General Orders, from Headquarters in New York, and in his Inaugural Address showed his concern that what happened in the U.S.A. had importance for liberty in "the whole world." Thomas Jefferson saw international meaning in the U.S. experiment in freedom and human rights; prophetically he wrote: "May it be to the world, what I believe it will be, (to some parts sooner, to others later, but finally to all,) the signal

of arousing men to burst [their] chains . . . and to assume the
blessings and security of self-government. . . . All eyes are . . .
opening to the rights of man."[7] Abraham Lincoln stressed the
world significance of the moral and political values of the U.S.A.:
in his Second Annual Message to Congress; in a celebration of
the Declaration of Independence at Philadelphia in 1861, at
which he said, "[the Declaration of Independence] gave liberty
not only to the people of this country, but hope to all the world,
for all future time"; and in his Second Inaugural Address,
beginning, "With malice toward none, with charity for all, with
firmness in the right as God gives us to see the right . . ."
concluding, "to do all which may achieve and cherish a just
and lasting peace among ourselves and with all nations."

The magnetism of such concern for human values has at-
tracted to our shores succeeding waves of immigrants and refugees.[8] Expressing the view of many, one of them, Albert Einstein, said: "Making allowances for human imperfections, I feel
that in America the most valuable thing in life is possible, the
development of the individual and his creative powers."[9] With
that whole historic backdrop, the drama of the American experiment of democracy in a world setting was carried forward
by the human rights initiatives of the Carter administration.
They reasserted world leadership of the U.S.A. in human rights
and proved to be a catalyst for increasing global concern and
action.

However, the U.S.A. faltered once more in the role of world
leader with the retreat of the Reagan administration which
abdicated its responsibility for human rights in both domestic
and foreign policy. This was seen by many observers at home
and abroad as defaulting on human values, human rights, and
human development as evidenced in statements, appointments,
and organizational and budget changes which deeply cut human
service programs and depreciated "mutual aid" for economic
and social development while vastly expanding military expenditures domestically and emphasizing them in "foreign aid."

In the matter of *apartheid,* the cruel and murderous denial
of human rights in southern Africa, including the problem of
Namibia, the U.S.A. has had a vacillating record, with recent
actions evidencing less critical concern. However, the churches,
in various ways, including communication with Christians in
South Africa, have sought to keep a focus on this issue and on

actions which might be taken. They have developed, among Protestant, Orthodox, and Roman Catholic groups, cooperative relationships and organizations and programs seeking more corporate responsibility in relation to their own and other investments and to the operation of banks and commercial enterprises doing business there.[10] In addition they have been seeking to have U.S. foreign policy for southern Africa be consistently concerned for the human rights and international problems there, supporting efforts in the UN, and seeking resolution of these problems by peaceful means as soon as possible.

A particular concern of the churches related to human rights and freedom is religious liberty.[11] There are problems in various areas of the world. Some have even been caused, at least in part, by some Christians seeking exclusive power or policies in a country or a culture. However, the most acute, persistent problems for decades have been in the U.S.S.R. and other Communist-dominated countries.[12] The churches' concerns, on the basis of principle, have encompassed not only Christians but also the rights and persons of other faiths including the Jews and the Muslims who have also suffered discrimination and persecution because of their religion. The churches have sought to publicize these problems, hoping that public opinion in the United States and other free countries would help to ameliorate them, and there have been some evidences of success from time to time. The churches have also made representations to the U.S. and other governments and have communicated their concerns to fellow Christian leaders in the U.S.S.R. and other Communist-dominated countries.

Human rights have been and continue to be a priority of the churches and Christians. They have acted because of biblical faith in a God concerned for freedom and for persons, and because of contemporary understanding of the basic rights in what it means to be human. The churches have given strategic leadership among NGOs on these issues. Once more they are marshaling their resources in the continuing struggle for human rights, feeling that the gains of centuries and of the last four decades must not be lost by discouragement or default. It is imperative that the churches and other organizations and Christians and other people, continue and intensify efforts in the U.S.A. and around the world, for increasing proclamation and practice of human rights, human values, and human development.

Relief, Rehabilitation, Refugees, and Immigration

While the subjects in this subsection are not usually prominent in U.S. foreign policy, they have been significant in the thinking and acting of the churches. So we stress them here.

U.S. policy has responded generously to needs for relief and rehabilitation in natural disasters around the world.

In policy and programs the U.S.A. has dealt on a massive scale with refugee problems around the globe. Occasional actions have been less than admirable, such as the treatment of Haitian refugees and not permitting boatloads of Jewish refugees from Nazi persecution to land in the U.S.A. But in general, since World War II with its millions of displaced persons, the U.S.A. has responded with substantial services to, and the resettlement of, refugees. The U.S.A. has given support to the worldwide program of the UN High Commissioner for Refugees.

Through the UN, 1981 was declared the International Year of Disabled Persons, to highlight their problems and to consider the nature and causes of their problems and constructive actions which can be taken to help the handicapped. The U.S.A. stressed such matters in recent years and so supported the declaration and its programs. However, in the same year the Reagan administration, in cutting budgets for human services, reduced programs for the handicapped.

On immigration policy, the U.S.A. has had a varied pattern. Earlier in this century the United States opened its gates to immigrants from Europe but held to a racist and discriminatory "Oriental Exclusion Act." The United States has adopted other misguided policies, such as "The Asia-Pacific Triangle" which blatantly discriminated against yellow and brown peoples of the world. A major codification of U.S. immigration laws in 1952 made some improvements but still retained many inequitable and discriminatory elements.

The churches have perennially given priority to immigration issues, even when others were unconcerned. They have done this on the basis of biblical injunctions from God to care for strangers and the dispossessed, and because of concern for equity and for persons.

The record of the churches on these issues is outstanding. They were honored for challenging and working to eliminate the "Oriental Exclusion Act." Interfaith cooperation of Protestant, Eastern Orthodox, and Roman Catholic churches and Jewish groups, following the 1952 codification, was a major force in bringing improvements. These made immigration laws less biased by race and national origin, eliminated "The Asia-Pacific Triangle," and set more equitable policies. The churches persevere in acting on immigration issues, such as those involving people from Mexico and Latin America, and programs for and with all migrant workers. Continued concern by churches and other organizations, Christians and other people, is needed to monitor immigration administration and policies to make them more equitable and concerned with human values and lives. The immigration administration and policies send messages to other peoples about the U.S.A. and in a race-conscious world affects our international relations and prospects for peace.

The UN and International Machinery

A crucial issue for U.S. foreign policy and for the present and the future of civilization, to which the churches have given persistent priority, is international organization. As this subject is so strategic for peace, we devote the next chapter to it.

Some Conclusions

Space precludes consideration of all the *many, varied* efforts of the churches to influence U.S. foreign policy to be more congruent with their values based on biblical, moral concerns.

In general overview, we observe that while the U.S. Government has stressed self-interest, as all nations do in a world of relative international anarchy, the churches consistently witness to a wider world perspective. When some people spoke of "The American Century," often chauvinistically, the churches stressed the sense of *responsibility* our nation should have and act upon for this changing planet. They continue to urge the U.S.A., as the most powerful, most wealthy nation on Earth, to formulate and implement its policies in ways that are good for our country but also beneficial to the world. This is in keeping with what Jesus said in Luke 12:48 about responsibility: "For unto whomsoever much is given, of him shall much be required" (KJV).

Seeking Peace Through the UN and International Machinery

... whatever we may have to go through now is less than nothing compared with the magnificent future God has in store for us.

(Romans 8:18, J. B. Phillips)

THE SCENE: A reception at the United Nations after the Hon. Adlai Stevenson had become the U.S. ambassador to the UN.

THE CAST OF CHARACTERS: Ambassador Stevenson, a small group of well-known international reporters, and the author.

THE SCRIPT: The reporters complained, gently, to the new U.S. ambassador that since he had come to the UN their job was difficult because there had not been much news for them to report. Stevenson responded that he understood their situation, realizing that a major criterion for news, as defined by the press, is "conflict." "However," he said, "my job is to minimize conflict and, insofar as possible, eliminate it. So, if I do my job well, it will make your job more difficult." The conversation continued, good-naturedly, with real empathy between the reporters and the ambassador, with his having clarified so concisely their relative roles and one of the major functions of the UN.

The ambassador had also pointed up the problem of the lack of news about the successes of the UN. We hear of the UN mostly only when there are crises, usually in the Security Council or the General Assembly. But only about 15 percent 121

of the UN's work is in political affairs and, of that, raw conflicts
are only a fraction. About 85 percent of the UN's budget, staff,
and operations deal with economic and social issues in "peace
building" around the world, not "conflict." Hence, little "news."
An article entitled "Spiking the UN,"[1] tells how press releases
about UN work are routinely stuck on a spike on editors' desks
and thus are not printed or broadcast.

So, the purpose of this chapter is to present a balanced picture
of the UN, explaining what it is and is not, some of its successes,
and its potentials. This is intended to give some brief historical,
theoretical, and political perspectives from a point of view of
Christian and church concerns.

As this is not a primer on the UN nor a what-now UN
information bulletin, both of which are important, the reader
is referred for them to the Notes,[2] the Bibliography, and the
Resources.

What the UN Is Not

Because many people do not know what the UN is not, they
blame it for not doing what they think it should, when that
may be neither realistic nor possible. Obviously, there are
reasons for criticism of the UN, which is necessary and can be
useful when done on a factual and constructive basis.[3] But
uninformed and cynical attacks on the UN can be destructive
to its present possibilities for peacekeeping and peace-building
and erosive of its potentials for the future of the human race.

People often ask in crises, "Why doesn't the UN do something?" The answer is fairly simple, in two parts: (1) It is often
doing "something"—and more than most people are aware of.
(2) When it is not doing "something," it is because the UN
member nations do not want to do something—and apart from
them, the UN has little power to act. Why? Because the major
powers set it up and maintain it that way. At the end of World
War II, they wanted an international organization with limited
authority. They were not willing to give up their sovereign
power to a world sovereign power. Hence the veto in the Security Council demanded by both the U.S.S.R. and the U.S.A.
and all the major powers. Hence, also, other limits on the UN.

The UN is not a World Government even though it has some
superficial appearances of one. The General Assembly looks
like a legislature, the Secretariat like an executive, and the

World Court like a judicial branch; but their powers are most minimal. (Besides, the use of the Court is almost infinitesimal.) In sum, the UN does not have the sovereignty, the authority, nor the coercive power of a government.

The UN is not a supranational organization. It is not, legally, above the major nations. It is less than they. In fact, it is their servant, to do their bidding. Some controls and coercion can be exercised, but only over smaller nations, by the major powers and others making up the Security Council.

The UN is not yet "a Parliament of man," nor "a Federation of the world," in the phrases of Tennyson.[4] Some, like the World Federalists, seek the goal of having the UN, as did the U.S., move from a weak, inadequate "confederation" to a strong, effective "federation" of the nations of the world.

In light of the realities stated here, Lord Caradon, when he was British ambassador to the UN, said, in amusement and in truth, "There is nothing wrong with the United Nations, only its members."

What the UN Is

Whether we like it or not, as noted in chapter 1, the basic unit in international relations is the sovereign nation state, and each seeks its own self-interest. So, the members see the UN as a combination of channels through which they can seek to promote their self-interest. They feel that it proves to be a desirable arrangement in which a member's self-perceived self-interest may coincide with the interests of most other states, or can be negotiated to the best mutual advantage.

So, the UN is "politics." Some complain about this. The story is told of a conversation in the U.S. Senate. One senator complained, "All they do at the UN is politics, politics, politics." The other replied, "And what do we do here?" "Politics" should not be thought of as a dirty word. Its honorable heritage goes back to Socrates, Plato, and Aristotle, who saw the *polis,* the government, as having basic responsibilities, as we noted earlier, for the good, the true, the beautiful, and the eternal in the life of the people. "Politics" is one of the chief ways in which society makes major moral decisions. It has to do with power: "Who gets what, when, how," as characterized by Harold Laswell.[5] At the UN these decisions are made by "politics" and diplomacy rather than by the destruction and death of war.

Thus, by peaceful means nations seek to enhance their power and self-interest, and those of allies, vis-à-vis other nations and groups.

And the UN is "problems." Some complain that these are all they ever hear about the UN. That one-sidedness comes, as we have seen, because of "news" conceived as "conflicts," ignoring larger numbers of solutions. But problems are precisely the reason for a world organization—to deal with global problems at the global level. Ambassador Stevenson used the analogy of a hospital. If there were no patients, there would be no need for a hospital. So with the UN: if there were no problems, there would be no need for it. Actually, the more problems there are, the more we need the UN, as a system for dealing with them.

The UN is a mirror of the world. Some complain about "the bad guys" being in it and wish for a club of just "us good guys." So small minorities seek to "get the U.S. out of the UN, and get the UN out of the U.S." But one of the values of the UN is that it mirrors the realities of the world, of the various nations' purposes and their power. Besides, nations may be able by associating to influence one another for the good of all.

Some Successes of the UN

On one side of the ledger of the record of the UN are many shortcomings, inadequacies, and failures. The list is long and important. But there is no need to repeat it here, because these failures have been so fully publicized. Such a catalog, however, should be checked against the facts, as to what the UN is and is not, what it can and cannot do, and the "political will" of the members which are "the United—more or less—Nations."

In the context of such realities, the successes of the UN are all the more remarkable. In the first chapter we saw that our world, internationally, has six major characteristics. Study shows that the UN has done significant work on each of them.

A continuous, silent success is the everyday work of the total UN system. Many of us like to use that term "UN system" because it gets beyond the narrow focus on crises, and it stresses the concept that along with the General Assembly and the Security Council, where most crises are dramatized, there are four other major organs—the Economic and Social Council, the Trusteeship Council, the Secretariat, and the International Court of Justice—and over twenty specialized agencies and programs. These are constantly at work during every one of the twenty-four hours, all around the globe, saving millions of lives every year, improving the quality of life for hundreds of millions of people, and helping to create "the conditions of peace."

In more specific terms, since its founding in 1945 the UN has been the instrument for preventing or stopping more than seventy wars. We are all duly thankful that there has not been a World War III, since it was common wisdom that war comes in cycles and we could expect one about every twenty years; yet it has been almost forty years since the last major war. Countless disputes have been settled. The importance of the UN's success in stopping or preventing minor wars and in settling disputes is that from such smaller beginnings, bigger wars have exploded in previous history. Terrorism has been reduced by international cooperation. Some steps have been taken in arms control, as noted earlier, with some of these agreements having direct or indirect relations to the UN. Economic and social development has been carried out on a much vaster scale than ever attempted in history. Relief, rehabilitation, and resettlement have been provided for tens of millions of refugees. Concern for the environment has been heightened and harnessed to specific programs for reducing pollution and providing cleaner air, water, and land for the peoples of Earth. Advances have been made in the problems and potentials of human habitats. Discrimination has been spotlighted and reduced in some areas of the globe. Some diseases, such as smallpox, have been virtually eliminated from the face of the earth; and others, such as malaria, have been dramatically reduced; encouraging progress has been made against other ills that have plagued humankind. The population explosion has been slightly dampened in many areas of the world and further progress is in sight. Human rights have been emphasized in articulation and in practice to degrees never before approached in history. Scores of millions of people have been lifted from illiteracy, and education has been promoted around the globe. And the list of successes could be extended with past and continuing ones.

It would be a mistake to give all the credit for all such progress to the UN, because individual nations, regions and other organizations all have played their parts. However, the

UN system has been involved significantly in most of the above successes. Its role in many has been so crucial that they could not have happened without the UN. The problems of the world have become so numerous, so vast, so complicated, and so all-involving of peoples around the world that the following is truer than ever: "If the UN did not exist, we would have to invent it."

The human meaning of many of the achievements of the UN, and some of the heroism and hope in them, was expressed by a person who gave twenty-seven years of his life to the UN and worked in more than seventy countries for economic and social development. He rose through the ranks of the Secretariat to become chief associate to Paul Hoffman in directing the UN Development Programme. After retirement from the UN, Clinton Rehling proved to be a superb teacher in higher education, with his concepts and concerns for a more humane and peaceful world. He shared some of his experiences with students in a "Human Hunger Awareness Week" at Trenton State College. He talked about his most difficult and his most interesting assignments. The author asked him, "What was your most satisfying experience?" Immediately he responded: "To think of the millions of people who are alive today who would have been dead if we had not done what we did through the UN."

The Churches and the UN

Not sufficiently known and appreciated, even among church people, are the roles, past and present, of Christianity and the churches in relation to the UN. The story is voluminous, as recorded in church archives. We touch on a few highlights here.

Even at first glance there is clear convergence of values and interests between Christianity as a universal religion and the UN as a universal organization, both seeking world peace. Universalism was one of the main concepts, as we have seen, in the Old Testament. In that spirit, Christians have interpreted a passage about common origin in God and the meaning of that for human relations among all peoples: "Have we not all one father? hath not one God created us? why do we deal treacherously every man against his brother . . .?" (Malachi 2:10, KJV). In the New Testament the concept of universalism of God and humankind is strongly stressed. For example, Paul in intellectual Athens declared the universalism of God and humanity, setting forth the Good News as making known the "unknown God": "God that made the world and all things therein . . . hath made of one blood all nations of men for to dwell on all the face of the earth . . ." (Acts 17:24-26, KJV).

On closer examination, we see a remarkable matching of ideas in Christianity and in the UN. Biblical faith, as we have seen, finds its basis in a universal God of love, a God of life, peace, justice, and freedom, who wills a more abundant life for the human family. The UN as a universal organization embodies strikingly parallel values, as set forth in its Charter:

> We the peoples of the United Nations determined to save succeeding generations from the scourge of war . . .
> to reaffirm faith in fundamental human rights . . .
> to establish conditions under which justice . . . can be maintained, and
> to promote social progress and better standards of life in larger freedom. . . . (from the Preamble)

Such parallels are more than coincidence. Some world leaders who helped shape the Charter were Christians whose faith was basic to their work. In its historical context, too, ideas from Western political philosophy and documents which were profoundly influenced by Christian thought were used in its development. Also, it reflects basic concepts which were developed by a deeply Christian philosopher, Immanuel Kant, in *Perpetual Peace.*[6] A Christian statesman, Woodrow Wilson, carried forward these ideas in his vision of the League of Nations which led to the UN.

Dedicated Christians were involved in founding and developing the UN. The Honorable Harold E. Stassen, the only surviving signer of the Charter for the U.S.A., is a committed Christian lay leader; he served with distinction as president of the American Baptist Convention. In succeeding years, in the UN, among the leading diplomats of the world, ambassadors and their staffs, and those serving in the UN Secretariat, there have been and are many consecrated Christians. Outstanding were Dag Hammarskjöld, secretary-general, who gave his life in the quest for peace, and Andrew W. Cordier, a leader in the Church of the Brethren, who served indefatigably as the assistant to several secretaries-general during the first sixteen

years of the UN. Others in the UN system have represented
different religions also emphasizing universalism and concomitant concerns for world organization and peace.

In addition to the leaders, millions of Christians in the U.S.A.
and around the world shared the same basic biblical faith,
believing in the universality of God and humanity and therefore supporting the idea of a universal organization, such as
the UN. Through extensive educational programs in countless
congregations, hosts of church members studied and saw clearly the significant parallels between their Christian faith and
the concepts of the UN. In the U.S.A., this was an instrumental
factor in a groundswell of opinion not only among church members but also in the general public, who were convinced of the
necessity for a universal organization and committed, from the
League of Nations experience, to see that the new venture
would not fail because of lack of U.S. participation. This tide
of public opinion with strong church leadership was an essential factor in the U.S. government's support for and participation in founding the UN.

The churches have an outstanding record in public support
for creating the UN, in direct influence in the shaping of its
Charter, in consultation on its operations, and in informed,
creative, critical support of its work.[7] The churches are among
the leaders in the nation in defending the UN under attacks
by extremists from time to time. Especially effective are the
nationwide efforts of Church Women United. Church leaders
did not fall into disillusionment with the UN. Having a realistic
view of the nature of humanity, society, and the organization,
they sought from the beginning to evaluate both the limitations
and the potentials of the UN. Through succeeding years, whether public opinion toward the UN was running hot or cold,
through various hate campaigns against the UN, and in face
of occasional U.S. administrations ignoring or depreciating the
UN, the churches have continued their enlightened, realistic,
steadfast support.

Many of the denominations, as well as the NCC, maintain
accredited representatives to the UN and to the U.S. Mission
to the UN. These representatives are important two-way communicators between the churches and the UN system. At the
global level, the WCC has an even closer relationship with the
UN, having consultative status. Thus, it can have more direct

influence on policies and programs in the UN. It has representatives present at all significant UN meetings around the world.
Its annual commentary on items in the General Assembly is
valuable for the use of ambassadors at the UN, UN staff, and
church groups around the world.

A dramatic move of the churches in relation to the UN was
the building of the Church Center for the UN at the UN Plaza
and 44th Street, facing the UN headquarters. With primary
leadership from the Methodist Church and the NCC, the member communions cooperated in 1962 in establishing the twelve-
story building as a center for programming related to the UN
and to peace. What has been achieved there is a major story
in itself. Here we summarize a few of its successes: It has
provided a center for coordinating the work of the churches,
and also other NGOs related to the UN system and peace; it
is the scene of UN seminars, which have brought as many as
forty thousand people a year from across the U.S.A. and around
the world; it has provided many kinds of Christian hospitality,
including worship, sacramental, pastoral, and educational programs for UN delegates, staff, their spouses and children, and
for countless other guests from overseas. It provides by its
presence a constant witness, to all who use its facilities and to
all who pass by and see it, that the churches have a basic
concern for the UN and for peace.

Need for Renewed and Greater Support for the UN and Other International Institutions

Starting with the Vietnam conflict, there has been a trend
in U.S. administrations, except in the Carter era, to revert to
older, more politicized patterns of "going it alone" on many
issues; of emphasizing bilateral rather than multilateral approaches on many matters, including foreign aid; of reem-
phasizing "power politics"; and of deemphasizing the UN and
other international organizations. This trend is all the more
ominous as it is becoming clear to increasing numbers of concerned people that international organization is one of the most
crucial questions of life or death for us and our descendants—
if we are to have any.

International organization, or its lack or inadequacy, is a
major factor among those which cause war or make for peace.
The case is clearly made in *Man, the State and War* by Kenneth

Waltz,[8] an uncommonly valuable work. Surveying philosophers and psychologists, he concludes that human nature does not make war inevitable, but that human capacities can be put into war or peace. He also concludes that the nation state does not make war inevitable, but that it can be mobilized for war or peace. Whence, then, comes war? A major factor is the lack of an international order or organization capable of bringing adequate control to international affairs. (Note world parallel to Hobbes's idea on the need, within a nation, for strong sovereignty to prevent a condition of war.)

Along with such theory, we have practical examples of the way international organization can help to prevent war and to bring the conditions of peace. Among these are regional organizations, of which the most impressive is the European Community (EC). Again, Christian lay persons, in politics and business, having a commitment to peace, were instrumental in founding it. They sought to make sure that Europe, the central precipitator of two world wars, would never again be so. Thus, they took practical steps to bind the peoples of Europe into interdependence, first economic, then political, in ways which would prevent war and promote peace. With all its problems, the EC continues to advance; it is now an economic-political force in the world, moving almost to the status of a superpower and revealing further potentials for peace and prosperity. It presents an exciting model of international organization, pointing some hopeful ways for the future of other regions, and with implications for world organization.

It is important that we pay more attention to "international machinery" of many kinds: regional arrangements within the UN system; those such as OAS (Organization of American States) and OAU (Organization for African Unity); regional banks; multinational corporations (in UN parlance, transnational); a wide range of NGOs, including union and trade organizations, cooperatives, environmentalists, scientists, and other professionals, women's organizations, the YMCA and YWCA, religious groups, others concentrating on the UN and on peace; and a vast, growing global network of countless international and regional organizations related to particular and general interests of the human race. The international network now includes at least 300 intergovernmental and at least 2,500 nongovernmental organizations.[9]

One crucial reason for supporting the UN and other international machinery, in addition to their vital importance in meeting present issues, is that they are a base on which to build the indispensable international structures for the future. At the center of it all, we desperately need the UN and such strengthening of it as may be feasible, as rapidly as possible.

The international structures for the future can fairly well be laid out on paper. For instance, the Clark-Sohn plan[10] has furnished such a global model. The major problem, given the present relative international anarchy, with all the issues of national sovereignty, power politics, lack of trust, differences of ideologies, and hostilities among particular nations and groups, is how we can go from here to there? How can we get from this largely unjust, often oppressive, quite inhumane, terror-filled "system," with its delicate "balance of power" to a new, more secure order of justice, freedom, and humanization?

Some propose revising the Charter, with sweeping reorganization of the UN. Most professionals argue that this is not politically possible now, that such an effort would result in a much lower order of international organization. Still, scholars and citizens should be thinking about the organizational changes that must be made eventually—and how we can achieve them.

Another approach is "functionalism."[11] This concept is that nations working together on a multitude of immediate issues can grow in habits of cooperation, in procedures to deal with diffferences, and in mutual confidence. Then they will be better able to work together on the more difficult issues. In the process, they can develop better international relations and structures. Thus, by incremental increasing of the use of international institutions, we can move forward toward more adequate world organization.

In order to eliminate war and make peace possible, it is imperative that a world international organization which will have adequate legislative, executive, and judicial powers be developed. This must be sufficient to channel conflicting national interests into peaceful processes, preserve the security, and enhance the potentials of all nations and peoples. This is essential if we are to survive and have an improving quality of life.

The UN is described by an outstanding diplomat, one of the

world's most eminent international lawyers, a national and world church leader, the Honorable Ernest A. Gross, as dealing with "the agenda of civilization."[12] Our time presses us all to think rationally and realistically, but also idealistically and with vision about the UN and other international machinery as custodians and evolving future carriers of "the agenda of civilization."

With such thinking, taking the long view forward, let us commit ourselves and our nations, insofar as we can, to critical, constructive support of the UN system and to the continuous quest for increasingly adequate international institutions. Let us work also to enhance the global network of organizations in the private sector, both business-related ones, corporations, labor, and cooperatives, and voluntary groups so that they may help all nations and peoples to be more creatively and constructively "bound in the bundle of the living" (to use a biblical phrase from 1 Samuel 25:29, about being bound with God).

Let us have the wit, the wisdom, the courage, and the perseverance to will and to work for a new world order: one under international law, with increasingly beneficial public and private institutions, to make for real and lasting peace with justice, freedom, and humanization.

As we "seek peace and pursue it" in this, as in the other ways we have considered together, we shall at times be faced with doubts, disappointments, and discouragements. However, we may take fresh courage, and find renewed faith, hope, and love in looking to the future which is in the providence of God. Thus, we extend from personal to global dimensions the epigraph with which we began our thinking in this chapter; ". . . whatever we may have to go through now is less than nothing compared with the magnificent future God has in store for us" (Romans 8:18, J. B. Phillips).

Acting for Peace:
Churches and People . . .
and You . . .?

. . . "Go and do likewise. . . ."
(Luke 10:37)

In 1964 the people of this land and the members of Congress needed to make decisions on a Civil Rights Act. These decisions were important for this country and also for international relations in a race-conscious world. A strategy was developed to combine the national and local forces of the churches to influence Congress in regard to this act. The strategy also included working with other significant NGOs. In the NCC, a dedicated young leader, Bob Spike, gave imaginative leadership, working with colleagues in a nationally directed program to focus on church and public opinion in local areas to influence the swing votes in the Senate and the House. Effort was concentrated not on those committed for or against the proposal but on those where such work might make a difference. This was in the Midwest and certain other selected states and congressional districts. National church leaders concentrated their efforts on consulting and communicating with senators and representatives in Washington and on mobilizing regional and local leaders to focus their work in the home territories of the swing persons in the Congress. So hosts of people and pastors in local congregations, alerted to the issue and convinced of its cruciality, communicated with their senators and representatives: delegations of informed Christians went to 133

Washington to meet with them and met with others in the home area when they came back to their constituencies; people who already knew their representatives well personally contacted them; others made contact via telephone calls, telegrams, letters, and postcards. Churches mobilized public opinion, using letters to the editor, TV and radio where possible, conversations, and phone calls to encourage neighbors, friends, and others to express their views to their senators and representatives. The successful result is history.

The Civil Rights Act of 1964 became the law of the land and a significant fact of life in the U.S.A. Obviously this was only one chapter in the civil rights movement. But it was a crucial one, helping to determine which way this nation would go and having strategic influences for the world. It reaffirmed a successful model for action by the churches for influencing public policy. And it was another in a long line of experiences demonstrating that the churches can make a difference in U.S. domestic and foreign policies.

One of the central figures in the history of civil rights and in the governmental part of the 1964 drama, Senator Hubert H. Humphrey, knowing the strategy the churches followed and seeing the results in votes in the Senate and House, said, in essence, "The churches made the difference. If it had not been for their work, we could not have achieved the victory."

On another occasion and issue, he also emphasized the crucial importance of the churches, this time in relation to foreign policy. He did this while chairing the Senate Foreign Relations Subcommittee on Disarmament when he introduced the author to give testimony on behalf of the churches. Senator Humphrey said that particular attention should be given to this part of the record because the churches have been consistently concerned for this issue and their leadership is crucial for disarmament.

Models of World, National, and Local Church Cooperation

In the churches' successful strategy on the Civil Rights Act we would emphasize the cooperation required at both national and local levels by church leaders and members.

In a parallel but different way cooperation for peace is operating among the churches at various levels all the time. A global model is working in "world ministries" and "service," as we noted, where church organizations are operating at the world, national, regional, and local levels. Missionaries, fraternal workers, service staff, and administrators at all levels are working in their places of responsibility; and members of local congregations are working there in programs and giving funds and goods to support the worldwide undertakings.

In "edu-action" for peace, national church leaders are observing developments in Washington and at the UN and are alerting their constituencies. They are consulting and otherwise communicating with senators, representatives, and key leaders in the administration, and in the international diplomatic community centering in the UN. They are testifying before congressional committees. They are also seeking to involve the resources of the mass media. Meanwhile, at the local level, church members are giving offerings which support these efforts of national programs and leaders in their denominations and in the NCC to bring Christian influence to bear on U.S. domestic and foreign policies. Their gifts also support the WCC in its global impact. Thus, more than is generally realized, people and pastors in the local churches by their budgets and offerings are helping to sustain strong and effective national and worldwide efforts for peace.

But more is needed. *The People, Yes.* That phrase says it; it is taken from the title of the book-long poem by Carl Sandburg[1] in which he declares his profound belief in democracy. Despite some political scientists' skepticism (and with good reason at times!) in saying, "the people, maybe," in the long run, for good or ill, this nation does operate on "the consent of the governed." So, what is desperately needed is for the people and pastors in local congregations across the land to continue to give and, indeed, to increase their offerings, which are important, but also to give their attention, time, thought, and deeds through programs of "edu-action" for peace. This will include, as happened in the Civil Rights Act strategy, their expressing their views, in every possible way, directly, to the decision makers in Washington. This communication is an important force in itself, and it will also give greater weight to the continuing contacts of church leaders with the public decision makers. The people of the local churches will also be doing all they can in their communities to influence public opinion so that their neighbors, friends, and others will also share in an increasingly powerful public opinion expressing specific concerns for peace. What is urgently needed is a rising tide of such thinking and action for peace—in villages, towns, cities, and states, all across this land and reaching Alaska and Hawaii, and back to Washington!

Programming in the Local Church

Programming for peace in the local church is, therefore, crucial to the national and world efforts of the churches. There already is in many local congregations, and needs to be in many more, a conscious focus on peace as a priority. This focus needs to be included in the total programming of the church: worship, education, and action.

Most churches in their worship do have Scripture readings, prayers, hymns, anthems, and occasional sermons on "peace." Christian churches, almost universally, have long and often been *speaking* "peace." But how many of them are actually *seeking* "peace"? There are all too few programs of education and action for peace.

Providentially, in this precarious period, vastly increasing numbers of local congregations will be cooperating with their denominations and the NCC in their *priority on peace* programs. We shall not go into details of all the myriad possibilities there are for study and action in the local church here, as this is not intended as a handbook. For such information, the reader is referred to her or his denomination, the NCC, and the WCC. These offer materials on issues, bulletins on actions, and general directions on programming to help the local congregation be as effective as it can, in itself, in its community, and as part of the growing national and world network of Christian peacemakers.[2]

Speaking of "priority on peace," the reader may wish to look at her or his local church to see how much of a "priority" peace really has there. For instance, what percentage of the budget is devoted to items for education and action for peace? Compare it, say, to the annual amount for flowers. Yes, flowers and other sundries have their place, but what about "the weightier matters" of peace, justice, and related concerns (cf. Matthew 23:23)? Or, again, in an inventory on time, what percentage of the reader's local church's total program during a week, a month, or a year is devoted to peace? Maybe, by careful planning, the reader, friends, and pastor could get more resources and dedicate more time for programs of "edu-action" for peace.

For Edu-action: "Things That Make for Peace"

Our first recommendation is that the reader and each local congregation seek guidance from her or his denomination, the NCC, and the WCC, as to the most significant, relevant issues at any given time, and materials related to "edu-action" on them.

A second recommendation is made to the reader and local congregations whose denominations may not have such programs. These persons may focus on issues which they see as most crucial, taking clues from chapters 6 and 7, relating their concerns to U.S. foreign policy, the UN, and other international organizations, so that their "edu-action" for peace is as relevant and effective as possible. Again, guidance may be gained from the NCC and the WCC.

It seems most strategic for local churches to concentrate their time and energies on such emphases as those suggested previously in the book. There will be groups and occasions in churches, however, which may furnish the opportunity to include other "things that make for peace" in a single program or a series of them. The following list is offered to suggest how wide-ranging and exciting the many issues are that "make for peace." Some of the items may, at first glance, not seem that relevant, but in the ways they can be developed, and keeping in mind the whole constellation of interrelated realities of "peace, justice, freedom, and humanization," it will be seen that all of these, and more, can be related as we "seek peace and pursue it." They are listed in alphabetical order, rather than priority of importance, because they vary in significance in different times and places.

COMMUNICATIONS—with freedom and general availability to people.

CULTURAL EXCHANGES—sharing in a spirit not so much of competition as of cooperation for the enrichment of all.

DEMOCRACY—its cultivation, improvement, and wider practice.

DEVELOPMENT—economic and social, including industrial *and* agricultural strategies.

DISARMAMENT—international *reduction* of *all* arms, leading to disarmament with universal security arrangements.

ECO-JUSTICE—a more equitable "New Economic Order," with fuller responsibilities for both developed and developing nations.

EDUCATION—including literacy, with opportunities for all to develop their capabilities, to benefit their lives and society.

ENERGY—emphasizing conservation, more efficiency, and exploration of increasing use of water, wind, and solar power.

ENVIRONMENT—stressing protection and improvement of the human ecosphere, with reverence for life in all its forms.

FAMILY LIFE—emphasizing cooperation, and nurture of persons concerned for others and for peace in the world.

FOOD—stressing increasing production, more equitable distribution for all persons, and maximum nutrition practices.

HEALTH—prevention of disease, protection and promotion of better health, with increasing services available.

HOSPITALITY—for international students and other people who are guests from different countries.

HOUSING—more adequate human habitations and settlements for all people in every land.

HUMAN RESOURCES—development of the most valuable of all resources, for the good of persons themselves and of the world.

HUMAN RIGHTS—promotion and practice of all rights—civil, political, economic, social, and cultural—for all people.

IMMIGRATION—legislation and administration with policies that are increasingly equitable, nondiscriminatory, and humane.

INTERNATIONAL ETHOS—Development of common, human-centered values, and a consequent growing sense of world community.

INTERNATIONAL INSTITUTIONS—supporting and developing the UN and other international institutions so that they are more adequate to serve as world-governing institutions eventually.

MISSION—supporting the world ministries of the church, with increasing spiritual, moral, and social development.

NATURAL RESOURCES—conservation and appropriate use, with more equitable compensation to people in developing areas.

POPULATION—reducing explosive growth by education, economic and social development, and responsible parenthood.

RACE RELATIONS—eliminating discrimination, direct and indirect, personal and institutional, and seeking a healthy multiracial society around the world.

REFUGEES—care and resettlement of these·persons, while seeking to eliminate the causes of such human displacement.

RELIEF AND REHABILITATION—more worldwide planning and services to victims of disasters and to the handicapped.

RELIGION—freedom of belief and practice, and encouraging world faiths in stressing universalism, global ethos, and world community.

SCIENTIFIC AND TECHNOLOGICAL DEVELOPMENT—for peaceful purposes, for enhancing human values and the quality of life.

SEAS—conservation, equitable laws, and just international arrangements for de-pollution, development, and use.

SEXUAL EQUALITY—improving attitudes, customs, and laws to eliminate discrimination, and to provide equal opportunities.

SOCIAL PROBLEM CONCERNS—to alleviate addiction to drugs, alcoholism, child abuse, crime, delinquency, and sexual assault.

SPACE—developing international cooperation to explore, exploit, and control the uses of space for peaceful purposes.

THEORY FOR INTERNATIONAL RELATIONS—more adequate for understanding and practicing peace, justice, freedom, and humanization.

TRANSPORTATION—improving systems; stressing mass transit and increasing availability; safeguarding from terrorism.

WORLD SERVICE—supporting these global ministries of the churches for relief, rehabilitation, economic and social development.

Programming with the Local Community: NGOs

A special recommendation to the reader and to pastors and people in local congregations is: It is important to be aware of and to cooperate with other responsible organizations beyond the walls of your church building, working for peace.[3] Approximately 150 of them cooperate at the national level through the United Nations Association of the U.S.A. in its Council of Organizations. Most of them have local chapters, branches, or groups in communities across the country. The local churches could greatly augment their own work for peace by sharing not only with the other churches in the community but also with other NGOs in programming for peace. On different occasions this may mean varying participation by the whole congregation or by a delegation or by individuals. In the author's field work in most of the fifty states in nationwide programs of Education and Action for Peace and in other experiences in working in international relations, he has observed that effective leaders for peace in the local congregations are usually also involved in other groups working for peace, such as local chapters of the UNA-USA, Councils on World Affairs, the League of Women Voters, labor unions, Coalitions for Nuclear Disarmament, some service clubs with special dedication to peace, such as certain Rotary and Zonta groups, the Junior Chamber of Commerce, Business and Professional Women, YMCA, YWCA, "Great Decisions Program" groups, and the UNICEF program.

The Ministry of the Laity for Peace

The church is not a building. The church is its members, and its activities are what they are doing during the days of the week. The services of worship and meetings in the church house are to "equip the saints," that is, to prepare the Christians to go out into their homes and vocations and social and civic life to do "the work of the ministry" to the world (Ephesians 4:10). Every day mothers, fathers, youth, and children in homes where peace is regarded as important, is taught and lived, are participating in myriads of ministries for peace. Obviously, this is where the future peacemakers of the world are being prepared. So this is one of the most significant ministries for peace. Then, there is peacemaking in the neighborhood and in the community. In their work, men and women have opportunities to be peacemakers among their colleagues; and, on a wider scale, many jobs and vocations have an indirect or a direct relation to working for world peace: for example, teachers and other educators, business persons, public administrators, politicians, lawyers, scientists, engineers, technicians, agricultural specialists, environmentalists, architects, artists, composers, musicians, authors, poets, playwrights, screenwriters, actors and actresses and others in the theatre and films, dancers, athletes, entertainers, people in the electronic and other mass media, including TV, radio, and the public prints, labor leaders, executives in trade associations, missionaries or fraternal workers, world service staff, pastors, and ecclesiastical bureaucrats. An almost endless list of types of work includes some kind of opportunities day by day to inch the world along at least a bit in the direction of peace, justice, freedom, and humanization.

People Acting for Peace in Special Ways

In addition to seeking peace in daily work, some men, women, youth, and children have taken on special projects for peace. Following are a few examples; they are actual people, all of them known personally to the author (except for TV interviewees), but names are not given for various reasons. One reason is that most of these models could be multiplied many times over; so the focus is not on the particular individuals but on the types of action. Do you know other peacemakers, such as the following?

A businessman in Iowa, president of a successful enterprise, dedicates 10 percent of his profits to work for peace. He also invests more than that percentage of his time in preparing and distributing materials, speaking, recording, broadcasting, and other services for peace.

A teacher in Washington, in Christian witness, used materials on global education for peace, wrote "letters to the editors" on the UN and peace, and distributed her own writings on peace.

A college student from Louisiana, attending a seminar at the Church Center for the UN, and then visiting the Senate Gallery, was deeply disturbed. A senator from his state was making a speech, offensive to other races, nations, and sensitive citizens. The student whispered, "Some day I will be speaking down here and I will be making sense." With Christian conviction, he set out on a career in politics in order to do peacemaking among races and nations.

Children in considerable numbers are now participating in demonstrations for disarmament and peace; an example was the largest rally ever held in New York, related to the UN

General Assembly Special Session on Disarmament. A little girl participating in the rally was interviewed on television. When asked why children were there, she replied, "We want to live to grow up."

A Christian layman, working in multinational corporate responsibilities from an industrial and financial base in Indiana, has given substantial leadership for economic development, educational progress, civil rights, advancement of architecture, music and other arts, and ethical concerns in business and government. Using his Greek New Testament, he has taught church school classes in his local congregation; he has served as president of the NCC and as a leader in the WCC. He has sought improvement for local communities, the country, and the world. Through his many, varied responsibilities he has made outstanding contributions to peace, justice, freedom, and humanization.

A husband and wife team in Connecticut led a church in sponsoring over thirty refugees and worked arduously to find them jobs and housing. Later, on a mission in higher education in Taiwan, the husband employed his skills from Harvard Business School and many years of experience to administer a college; his wife made their home a center of Christian love and international understanding.

A woman from California, after participating in a UN seminar at the Church Center for the UN, persuaded a local newspaper publisher to change its policy from anti-UN to fairness.

A church leader who served in world missions and evangelism in thirty countries and who is now leading groups in the U.S.A. has special programs and offerings to "seek peace and pursue it."

A reporter on a newspaper in Connecticut seeks special opportunities to write articles dealing with religion and peace.

A woman in New Jersey, the wife of a leading pastor, has given significant leadership at the state level in organizing Christian efforts for peace and justice.

The chief executive of MacDonnell-Douglas Aircraft Corporation, in Missouri, pioneered in planning with the workers for them to have a new annual holiday with pay, UN Day, October 24, to stress the importance of international organization and peace.

A wife and husband from Missouri, in Christian commitment, planned with church leaders and gave funds for a Dahlberg Peace Award to be given at each national convention of the American Baptist Churches to highlight outstanding achievement for peace.

The mayor of Princeton, New Jersey, led in the community's observation of UN Day, inviting UN delegates from other lands. More than fifty, with their families, came to celebrate in Princeton University Chapel and stay the weekend in homes, experiencing warm hospitality, life in this country, and mutual understanding for peace.

A student from California attended a seminar at the Church Center for the UN, which contributed to his career and helped him to advance through local to national UNA-USA work for peace.

A husband and wife team, in addition to outstanding national denominational leadership, served in the ecumenical movement in the NCC and the WCC, then in international ministries at the American Church in Paris, always pursuing peace.

A Christian family, mother, father, and three children, in New Jersey gave to "world ministries" in church offerings every week, gave clothing and money to "world service," and discussed and acted for peace: for example, participated in "Trick or Treat" and Greeting Cards for UNICEF to help other children; led in "edu-action" and Church Women United projects; served in national and overseas programs for peace.

... And You ...?

Now, about that question, "But what can I do for peace?" Building on the many examples in this book, a miscellaneous, roundup list[4] may help to dispel any lingering doubt the reader may have as to whether you can do "things that make for peace." Pray for peace. Worship, using materials on peace. Meditate on peace; use the Bible, poems, drama, and other writings on peace. Work with others to collect war toys and then destroy them because of their negative influence. Make banners for peace for the church, home, and elsewhere. Send greetings of peace. Sing and play music with messages for peace. (And discourage the use of warlike hymns.) Give your self; then give thought, time, talents, food, goods, animals, poultry, grain, seeds, and funds for "world ministries," "world service," and other projects that "make for peace." Support and

share in "edu-action" and other programs for peace in your
local church. Communicate with government leaders in the
administration, e.g., the president, the secretary of state, the
secretary of defense, and other cabinet members, including the
U.S. ambassador to the UN, the head of the Arms Control and
Disarmament Agency. Use the phone, telegrams, letters, postcards; with your senators and representatives use those means
plus personal and group consultations, in Washington, and in
your own area when he or she comes home to meet with con-
stituents. Write "letters to the editor," also to your radio and
TV stations. Talk with others about peace. Be active in other
NGOs as part of the larger, growing world network for peace.

About the disclaimer, "But I am just one person;" recall:

I am only one person. But I am one.
I cannot do everything. But I can do something.
What I can do, I must do. What I must do, I will do.

Now you might expect to read, "In conclusion of this 'joint
venture' . . ." But not so; *this is the beginning of the rest of our
life as we "seek peace and pursue it."*

When Jesus was discussing the meaning of "love thy neighbor," he said, "Go and do likewise." We have seen churches
and people in effective study and action for peace, justice,
freedom, and humanization. With such examples of worldwide
ways of "loving thy neighbor," we would say "Godspeed" in our
quest for peace, in the words of Jesus:

"Go and do likewise."

Notes

(Books of particular relevance are noted with an asterisk.)

PROLOGUE

¹Ralph Waldo Emerson, *Society and Solitude,* "Success" (Boston: Fields, Osgood, & Co., 1870), pp. 264-265.

²Gian Cărlo Menotti, Commencement, Westminster Choir College, Princeton University Chapel, May 11, 1981.

CHAPTER 1

¹Robert L. Heilbroner, *An Inquiry into the Human Prospect* (New York: W. W. Norton & Company, Inc., 1974), p. 13.

* ²Jonathan Schell, *The Fate of the Earth* (New York: Alfred A. Knopf, Inc., 1982), esp. pp. 54-96.

³*Ibid.,* p. 57.

⁴*Ibid.,* p. 58.

⁵*Ibid.,* p. 65.

⁶*Ibid.,* p. 72.

⁷*Ibid.,* pp. 93-94.

⁸*Ibid.,* pp. 95-96.

⁹Stan Kossen, *The Human Side of Organizations,* 2nd. ed. (New York: Harper & Row, Publishers, Inc., 1978), p. 448, re a presentation by Dr. William G. Pollard, nuclear physicist and Episcopal priest.

¹⁰See philosophical roots in Niccolò Machiavelli, *The Prince* and *The Discourses* (New York: The Modern Library, 1940).

¹¹*New York Times,* November 6, 1981, p. A13.

¹²The first monumental study: Quincy Wright, *A Study of War* (Chicago: University of Chicago Press, 1942). An interesting forerunner: *The Causes of War, Economic, Industrial, Racial, Religious, Scientific and Political* (New York: Macmillan, Inc., 1932). Contributions of leaders of the World Conference for International Peace Through Religion.

¹³*UNESCO Yearbook on Peace and Conflict Studies 1981.* UN Educational, 145

Scientific and Cultural Organization (Westport, Conn.: Greenwood Press, 1983).

CHAPTER 2

[1]"The Soldier's Prayer" of General George S. Patton, in H. Essame, *Patton: A Study in Command* (New York: Charles Scribner's Sons, 1974), p. 253. cf. "The War Prayer" of Mark Twain, in *Europe and Elsewhere* (New York: Harper & Row, Publishers, Inc., 1923), pp. 394 ff.

[2]Erik Karlfeldt, Swedish poet, quoted on Hammarskjöld's induction as UN Secretary-General, in Henry P. Van Dusen, *Dag Hammarskjöld, the Statesman and His Faith* (New York: Harper & Row, Publishers, Inc., 1967), p. 127.

[3]See references in later Notes and Bibliography.

[4]In the Hebrew text, YHWH; some rendered it JHVH, so translated it "Jehovah"; more generally, YHWH and "Yahweh"; translated by KJV and RSV as "LORD".

[5]In the Old Testament it is used more than 200 times. Some later uses may mean "heavenly hosts," but "the earliest meaning ... clearly associates God with the armies of Israel" (Peter C. Craigie, *The Problem of War in the Old Testament* [Grand Rapids, Mich.: Wm. B. Eerdmans Publishing Company, 1978], p. 36).

[6]*The Interpreter's Bible* (Nashville: Abingdon Press, 1953), vol. 2, p. 871. See Craigie, *op.cit.*, Appendix, pp. 115-122. On one point in chapter 4, his argument not to use the term "'Holy' War" is not persuasive to this author; so we use it, as do a number of scholars.

[7]See, in addition to Craigie: Vernard Eller, *War and Peace from Genesis to Revelation* (Scottdale, Pa.: Herald Press, 1981).

Millard Lind, *Yahweh Is a Warrior: The Theology of Warfare in Ancient Israel* (Scottdale, Pa.: Herald Press, 1980).

Patrick D. Miller, *The Divine Warrior in Early Israel* (Cambridge, Mass.: Harvard University Press, 1973).

Rudolf Smend, *Yahweh War and Tribal Confederation*, trans. Max G. Rogers (Nashville: Abingdon Press, 1970).

J. Swaim, *War and Peace in the Bible* (Maryknoll, N.Y.: Orbis Books, 1982).

G. Ernest Wright, *The Old Testament and Theology* (New York: Harper & Row, Publishers, Inc., 1969).

[8]Thomas à Kempis, *The Imitation of Christ*, trans. Richard Whitford (New York: Washington Square Press, Inc., 1953), p. 261.

[9]Albert Schweitzer, *Out of My Life and Thought* (New York: Holt, Rinehart and Winston, Inc., New American Library, 1933), p. 126. See also his *Reverence for Life*, trans. Reginald H. Fuller (New York: Harper & Row, Publishers, Inc., 1969).

[10]See primitive paintings by Edward Hicks (1780–1849) of Newtown, Pennsylvania, who did more than fifty versions of "The Peaceable Kingdom" based on Isaiah, with peaceful animals in the foreground and William Penn's Peace Treaty with the Indians in the background.

[11]See Charles Rann Kennedy's play "The Terrible Meek" (New York: Samuel French, Inc., 1912), p. 39. At the cross, a captain says to Jesus' mother: "I tell you, woman, this dead son of yours, disfigured, shamed, spat upon, has built a kingdom this day that can never die. ... The earth is *his* and he made it. He and his brothers ... are the only ones who ever really did possess it: not the proud: ... not the vaunting empires of the world. Something has happened up here on this hill to-day to shake all our kingdoms of blood and fear to the dust. ... The meek, the terrible meek, the fierce agonizing meek, are about to enter their inheritance."

* [12]G. H. C. Macgregor, *The New Testament Basis of Pacifism* (New York: The Fellowship of Reconciliation, 1936).

* Richard McSorley, *The New Testament Basis of Peacemaking* (Center for Peace Studies, Georgetown University, 1979).

* John Howard Yoder, *The Politics of Jesus, vicit Agnus noster* (Grand Rapids, Mich.: Wm B. Eerdmans, 1972).

CHAPTER 3

[1]John Greenleaf Whittier, "Dear Lord and Father of Mankind," from "The Brewing of Soma," *Masterpieces of Religious Verse,* ed. James Dalton Morrison (New York: Harper & Row, Publishers, Inc., 1948), sel. 746.

[2]B. J. Diggs, ed., *The State, Justice, and the Common Good,* An Introduction to Social and Political Philosophy (Glenview, Ill.: Scott, Foresman & Company, 1974), pp. 30-31. Original source: *Leviathan,* XIV and XV.

[3]See various expressions of this in *Love and Justice: Selections from the Shorter Writings of Reinhold Niebuhr,* ed. D. B. Robertson (Magnolia, Mass.: Peter Smith, 1976).

[4]A. J. Muste, *The World Task of Pacifism* (Wallingford, Pa.: Pendle Hill Publications, 1941). _____, *War Is the Enemy* (Wallingford, Pa.: Pendle Hill Publications, 1942).

[5]Paul Tillich, *Love, Power, and Justice,* Ontological Analyses and Ethical Applications (New York: Oxford University Press, 1954), pp. 62-71.

[6]John Rawls, *A Theory of Justice* (Cambridge, Mass.: Belknap Press of Harvard University Press, 1971), pp. 11, 60; developed in chaps. 2 and 3, pp. 54-192.

[7]Raymond D. Gastil, "The Comparative Survey of Freedom in the Tenth Year," *Freedom at Issue,* No. 64 (Jan.–Feb. 1982), pp. 3–20.

[8]*New York Times,* 11/5/81.

[9]L. S. Stavrianos, *The Promise of the Coming Dark Age* (San Francisco: W. H. Freeman & Company, 1976).

[10]Diggs, *op. cit.,* p. 45.

[11]P.B.S. interview 11/8/81. See also: Noam Chomsky, *Language and Mind* (New York: Harcourt, Brace Jovanovich, Inc., 1968), enlarged edition pp. xi, 1, 65-66; *Problems of Knowledge and Freedom* (New York: Vintage Books, 1971); *Towards a New Cold War,* Essays on the Current Crisis and How We Got There (New York: Pantheon Books, 1982).

[12]"An invasion of armies can be resisted, but not an idea whose time has come," Victor Hugo, translated into English from *Histoire d'un Crime.* John Bartlett, *Familiar Quotations* (Boston: Little, Brown and Company, 1882, 15th ed., 1980), p. 491.

[13]Constantinos Apostolos Doxiadis, *ACTION for Human Settlements* (New York: W. W. Norton & Company, Inc., 1977), p. 125. See also *Anthropopolis: City for Human Development* (New York: W. W. Norton & Company, Inc., 1975), pp. 19, 46-100. He uses "anthropos" to mean "human being" to avoid male overtones of the English word "man." The "polis" was the city-state, hence, used to mean "government."

Among the Greeks' human concerns, some wanted an end to war. Aristophanes proposed in 411 B.C. an ingenious way in his play, "Lysistrata": She led the women of Greece in a sex strike until the men would make peace in the Athens-Sparta war. In the play, the men capitulated and made peace.

[14]*Heauton Timorumenos,* I.i.25. cited in *The Oxford Dictionary of Quotations* (London: Oxford University Press, 1953), p. 541.

[15]Diggs, *op. cit.,* p. 38.

[16]*Ibid.*, pp. 35 ff. and selections from Locke's *Two Treatises of Government,* in Diggs, *op. cit.*, pp. 67 ff.

[17]*Ibid.*, p. 33; a summary of Locke's thinking is expressed in the *Second Treatise,* chap. 9, para. 128.

* [18]*The Quest for Peace,* The Dag Hammarskjöld Memorial Lectures, ed. Andrew W. Cordier and Wilder Foote (New York: Columbia University Press, 1965), p. 315.

* [19]See *United Nations Action in the Field of Human Rights* (UN 1979). It reviews activities of the UN in this field from the establishment of the UN in 1945 to December 31, 1977.

[20]Andrew Young in film *I Want to Live,* Church World Service.

[21]Abraham H. Maslow, *Motivation and Personality* (New York: Harper & Row, Publishers, Inc., 1954), chap. 5, "A Theory of Human Motivation," pp. 80-106.

[22]Paul L. Lehmann, *Ethics in a Christian Context* (New York: Harper & Row, Publishers, Inc., 1963), p. 117.

[23]Final phrase in "Violence, Nonviolence and the Struggle for Social Justice," a statement commended by the Central Committee, WCC, 1973, for study, comment, and action.

[24]Pierre Teilhard de Chardin, *Hymn of the Universe,* trans. Gerald Vaun (London: Collins, Fontana Books, 1970), pp. 77, 106.

[25]Emil Brunner, *The Divine-Human Encounter,* trans. A. W . Loos (Philadelphia: The Westminster Press, 1943), pp. 84-89, 90, 103-104. Martin Buber, *I and Thou,* trans. R. G. Smith (Edinburgh: T. & T. Clark, 1937).

[26]Edwin Markham, "Live and Help Live," in *Masterpieces of Religious Verse,* sel. 1544.

[27]Edwin Markham, "Man-Making,"*ibid.*, sel. 1377.

[28]Protagoras, *Fragment 1,* John Bartlett, *op. cit.*, p. 78.

CHAPTER 4

* [1]Gene Outka, *Agape, An Ethical Analysis* (New Haven: Yale University Press, 1972), p. 1.

[2]Joseph Henry Thayer, trans., *A Greek-English Lexicon of the New Testament, being Grimm's Wilke's Clavis Novi Testamente* (New York: Harper & Row, Publishers, Inc., 1881), p. 322.

* [3]Anders Nygren, *Agape and Eros, A Study of the Christian Idea of Love.* Part I. Authorized translation by A. G. Hebert, M.A. (New York: The Macmillan Co., 1932, reprinted, 1937).

[4]Paul Tillich, *Love, Power, and Justice* (New York: Oxford University Press, 1954), pp. 28-29, 67, 70, 114-115, 122.

[5]Outka, *op. cit.*, esp. pp. 207-309.

[6]*Reinhold Neibuhr on Politics,* ed. Harry R. Davis and Robert C. Good (New York: Charles Scribner's Sons, 1960), p. 136.

[7]The Fellowship of Reconciliation, in the U.S.A. and in its International Fellowship, is an outstanding example. Also worthy of special note are the "pacifist fellowships" or "peace fellowships" in various denominations.

CHAPTER 5

[1]Kenneth Scott Latourette, *A History of the Expansion of Christianity,* 7 vols. (New York: Harper & Row, Publishers, Inc., 1937–1945).

[2]Albert Schweitzer, *Out of My Life and Thought* (New York: Holt, Rinehart and Winston, Inc., New American Library, 1933), p. 128.

[3]Clarence Jordan, *The Cotton Patch Version of Hebrews and the General*

Epistles. A colloquial translation with a Southern accent. (New York: Association Press, 1973).

⁴Dag Hammarskjöld, *Markings* (New York: Alfred A. Knopf, Inc., 1964), p. 122.

⁵John Macmurray, *Reason and Emotion* (London: Faber & Faber Limited, 1962), p. 86.

CHAPTER 6

¹Helmut Richard Niebuhr, *Christ and Culture* (New York: Harper & Row, Publishers, Inc., 1956).

²Jonathan Schell, *The Fate of The Earth* (New York: Alfred A. Knopf, Inc., 1982).

* ³Ruth Leger Sivard, *World Military and Social Expenditures, 1982* (Leesburg, Va.: World Priorities, 1982). p. 26.

⁴Michael R. Gordon, "Arms and Inflation," *New York Times,* April 2, 1981, p. 27.

⁵*Book of World Rankings,* ed. George Thomas Kurian (New York: Facts on File, Inc., 1979), p. 62.

⁶*The Pittsburgh Press,* August 24, 1977.

⁷Thomas Jefferson, "Letter to Roger C. Weightman," in *The Portable Thomas Jefferson,* ed. Merrill D. Peterson (New York: The Viking Press, 1975), p. 585.

⁸John F. Kennedy, *A Nation of Immigrants* (New York: Harper & Row, Publishers, Inc., 1964).

⁹From a poster in the series "Great Ideas of Western Man."

¹⁰Interfaith Center on Corporate Responsibility. Room 566, Interchurch Center. 475 Riverside Drive, N.Y., NY 10027.

¹¹For example, O. Frederick Nolde, *Free and Equal* (Geneva: World Council of Churches, 1967).

¹²*Religion in Communist Dominated Areas,* ed. Blahoslav Hruby. 10 issues per year. 475 Riverside Drive, N.Y., NY 10027.

CHAPTER 7

¹"*Spiking the UN,*" by Oliver Jackman, former Barbados ambassador to the UN and journalist, *New York Times* (October 11, 1971).

* ²The best *brief* summary of history, structure, accomplishments, and misconceptions about the UN: "ABC'S OF THE UN," folder published by UNA-USA and National Education Association.

For current information on the UN: publications of the WCC, NCC, denominations; and UNA-USA. Excellent source for keeping *au courant* on the UN and related matters: *The Inter Dependent,* 10/yr., UNA-USA jointly with Overseas Development Council and Experiment in International Living. See also UNA-USA Policy Studies published occasionally.

³See critique by UN Secretary-General Perez de Cuellar, reported in Bernard D. Rossetes, "Perez de Cuellar Concedes the U.N. Is Being Ignored," *New York Times* (September 8, 1982).

⁴Alfred Lord Tennyson, "Locksley Hall," in *The Poetical Works of Tennyson* (New York: Hurst and Company, Publishers, n.d.) p. 94.

⁵Harold D. Laswell, *Who Gets What, When, How* (New York: McGraw-Hill, Inc., 1936).

* ⁶Immanuel Kant, *Perpetual Peace* (1795). Introduction by Nicholas Murray Butler (New York: Columbia University Press, 1939).

⁷A major architect in the churches' relations with the UN was Walter W.

Van Kirk, 1931–1956. Executive Director, Department of International Affairs, Federal Council of Churches, then, of the NCC. He made history, but he also looked to the future as suggested in title of one of his books, *Religion and the World of Tomorrow* (Chicago: Willett, Clark & Co., 1941).

[8]Kenneth Waltz, *Man, the State and War* (New York: Columbia University Press, 1959).

Another relevant book: Richard E. Leakey and Roger Lewin, *People of the Lake: Mankind and Its Beginnings* (New York: Anchor/Doubleday & Co., Inc., 1978). It rejects the idea that *homo sapiens* descended from "killer apes" wielding weapons as "warriors," as a genetic phenomenon; it discredits the idea that human nature makes war inevitable; it asserts that what made mankind unique is the ability to cooperate; that constructive cooperation is primary and basic to humankind; war is secondary and cultural.

[9]A. LeRoy Bennett, *International Organizations, Principles and Issues*, 2nd. ed. (Englewood Cliffs, N.J.: Prentice-Hall, Inc., 1980), p. 9.

[10]Grenville Clark and Louis B. Sohn, *World Peace Through World Law* (Cambridge, Mass.: Harvard University Press, 1958).

[11]Ernst B. Haas, *Beyond the Nation-State: functionalism and international organization* (Stanford, Calif.: Stanford University Press, 1964).

[12]Ernest A. Gross, *United Nations, Structure for Peace* (New York: Harper & Row, Publishers, Inc., 1962).

CHAPTER 8

[1]Carl Sandburg, *The People, Yes* (New York: Harcourt Brace Jovanovich, Inc., 1936).

[2]Additional resources with valuable, practicable ideas:
* John Donaghy, *Peacemaking and the Community of Faith*, A Handbook for Congregations (Nyack, N.Y.: Fellowship of Reconciliation, 1982).
* Barton and Dorothy Hunter, *Building Peace*, Suggestions for Church and Community (New York: Friendship Press, 1976).
* Betty Reardon, *Militarization, Security, and Peace Education* (Valley Forge: United Ministries in Higher Education, 1982).

[3]An insightful study by an NGO leader: Dorothy Robins, *Experiment in Democracy: The Story of the U.S. Citizens Organizations in Forging the Charter of the United Nations* (West Linn, Oreg.: Parkside Press, 1971).

For the historic importance of voluntary organizations in the U.S.A. see: Alexis de Tocqueville, *Democracy in America* (1835), new translation by George Lawrence (New York: Harper & Row, Publishers, Inc., 1966).

[4]Thanks for the idea of such a list and some of its items to Olive Tiller, a leader in the Baptist Peace Fellowship.

Bibliography

This is a selective rather than a comprehensive listing of books, periodicals, a bulletin, and a directory which have been of interest to the author in work for peace. Some books are included because they are valuable but are not found on usual lists. Some items out of print may be found in libraries or book shops. Books in the Notes of particular relevance are noted with an asterisk; while not listed here, they are part of this book's bibliography.

Anderson, Bernhard W., *The Living Word of the Bible*. Philadelphia: The Westminster Press, 1979.

Bainton, Roland H., *Christian Attitudes Toward War and Peace: a historical survey and critical reevaluation*. Nashville: Abingdon Press, 1980.

Ball, George W., ed., *Global Companies: The Political Economy of World Business*. Englewood Cliffs, N.J.: Prentice-Hall, Inc., 1975.

Barnes, Roswell P., *Under Orders; the churches and public affairs*. New York: Doubleday & Co., Inc., 1961.

Bennett, John C., and Seifert, Harvey, *U.S. Foreign Policy and Christian Ethics*. Philadelphia: The Westminster Press, 1977.

Bonhoeffer, Dietrich, *Ethics*. Edited by Eberhard Bethge. Trans. Neville Horton Smith. New York: Macmillan, Inc., 1965.

Brewer, Thomas L., *American Foreign Policy: A Contemporary Introduction*. Englewood Cliffs, N.J.: Prentice-Hall, Inc., 1980.

Brunner, Emil, *The Divine Imperative*. A study in Christian ethics. Philadelphia: The Westminster Press, 1979.

Butterfield, Herbert, *International Conflict in the Twentieth Century: A Christian View*. Westport, Conn.: Greenwood Press, 1960.

Cavert, Samuel McCrae, *The American Churches in the Ecumenical Movement, 1900–1968*. Wilton, Conn.: Association Press, 1968.

Claude, Inis L., Jr., *Swords into Plowshares: The Problems and Progress of International Organization*. New York: Random House, Inc., 4th ed. 1971.

Cordier, Andrew W., and Maxwell, Kenneth L., eds., *Paths to World Order*. 2nd Hammarskjöld Lectures. New York: Columbia University Press, 1967.

Cousins, Norman, *In Place of Folly*. New York: Washington Square Press, 1962.

Fagley, Richard M., *The Population Explosion and Christian Responsibility*. New York: Oxford Press, 1960.

Falk, Richard A., *A Study of Future Worlds*. New York: The Free Press, 1975.

Frank, Jerome D., *Sanity and Survival: Psychological Aspects of War and Peace*. New York: Random House, Inc., 1968.

Gremillion, Joseph, *The Gospel of Peace and Justice: Catholic Social Teaching Since Pope John*. Maryknoll, N.Y.: Orbis Books, 1976.

Hoffman, Paul G., *World Without Want*. Westport, Conn.: Greenwood Press, 1962.

IMPACT. Interreligious action network sponsored by Protestant, Catholic, and Jewish agencies. Approximately 20 mailings per year.

Kaplan, Morton A., *On Freedom and Human Dignity: The Importance of the Sacred in Politics*. Morristown, N.J.: General Learning Corporation, 1973.

Laqueur, Walter, and Rubin, Barry, eds., *The Human Rights Reader*. Philadelphia: Temple University Press, 1979.

Moltmann, Jurgen, *The Theology of Hope*. New York: Harper & Row, Publishers, Inc., 1967.

Nelson, Jack A., *Hunger for Justice: The Politics of Food and Faith*. Maryknoll, N.Y.: Orbis Books, 1980.

Padelford, Norman, Lincoln, George A., and Olvey, Lee D., *The Dynamics of International Politics*. New York: Macmillan,

Inc., 3rd. ed., 1976.

Plano, Jack C., and Olton, Roy, *International Relations Dictionary*. Santa Barbara, Calif.: ABC-Clio, 1982.

Rauschenbusch, Walter, *Prayers of the Social Awakening*. Folcroft, Pa.: Folcroft Library Editions, 1909.

"Register Citizen Opinion" annual directory, through denominations.

Thompson, Kenneth W., *Christian Ethics and the Dilemmas of Foreign Policy*. Durham, N.C.: Duke University Press, 1959.

Tinbergen, Jan, *The Rio Report: Reshaping the International Order*. 3rd. Report of the Club of Rome. New York: Signet, 1977.

Ward, Barbara, *Progress for a Small Planet*. New York: W. W. Norton & Co., Inc., 1979.

West, Charles C. *The Power to Be Human: Toward a Secular Theology*. New York: Macmillan, Inc., 1971.

PERIODICALS AND JOURNALS

America

American Behavioral Scientist

American Political Science Review

Bulletin of the Atomic Scientists

Christian Century

Christianity and Crisis

Commentary

Fellowship

Foreign Affairs

Foreign Policy

Inter Dependent

International Organization

International Studies Quarterly

Journal of Conflict Resolution

Journal of International Affairs

Orbis

Perspective

Political Science Quarterly

Religion in Communist Dominated Areas

The Monthly UN Chronicle

World Politics

Worldview

The Yale Journal of World Public Order

Also see Periodicals of:
   World Council of Churches
   National Council of Churches
   Denominations
   Denominational Peace Groups

RESOURCES FOR PROGRAMMING FOR PEACE

Among myriad resources, these as well as denominational agencies have been found by the author to be of special value:

Commission of the Churches on International Affairs, 777 United Nations Plaza, NY, NY 10017

National Council of Churches, 475 Riverside Dr., NY, NY 10027

Church Women United, 475 Riverside Dr., NY, NY 10027

American Friends Service Committee, 1501 Cherry St., Philadelphia, PA 19102

Churches' Center for Theology and Public Policy, 4500 Massachusetts Ave., NW, Washington, DC 20016

Council on Religion and International Affairs, 170 E. 64th St., NY, NY 10021

Fellowship of Reconciliation, Box 271, Nyack, NY 10960

Friends Committee on National Legislation, 245 Second St., N.E., Washington, DC 20002

Foreign Policy Association, ("Great Decisions Program," *Headline Series,* etc.), 205 Lexington Ave., NY, NY 10016

Institute for World Order, 777 UN Plaza, NY, NY 10017

Interfaith Center on Corporate Responsibility, 475 Riverside Dr., Rm. 566, NY, NY 10115

League of Women Voters, 1730 M St., N.W., Washington, DC 20036

National Education Association, 1201 16th St., N.W., Washington, DC 20036

National Interreligious Service Board for Conscientious Objectors, 550 Washington Bldg., 15th and NY Ave., N.W., Washington, DC 20005

UN Office for Public Information, United Nations, NY, NY 10017

United Nations Association of the USA, 300 E. 42nd St., NY, NY 10017

U.S. Committee for UNICEF, 331 E. 38th St., NY, NY 10016

Women's International League for Peace and Freedom (U. S. Section), 1213 Race St., Philadelphia, PA 19107

Index